# THE ECONOMICS OF SOUL PURPOSE

# THE ECONOMICS OF SOUL PURPOSE

## From Passion to Productivity

THE ACCREDITED NETWORK

www.theaccreditednetwork.com

The Accredited Network Publishing
9890 South 300 West Suite 300
Sandy, UT 84003
www.theaccreditednetwork.com

Book cover design, interior layout and design: Brand Alchemy Group. Contact–
*phone:* 801-304-7746 *email:* studio@brandalchemygroup.com

ISBN- 9780979623615

PRINTED IN USA

TABLE OF CONTENTS

# TABLE OF CONTENTS

# MAXIMIZING SOUL PURPOSE

I recently completed my first triathlon. It was both a humbling and inspiring experience. I was humbled the first time I got into the swimming pool to begin my training, and was told by my coach that the "Doggy Paddle" was not the most efficient stroke to use over a one-half mile course. I was inspired, however, that after two months of intensive training I was able to swim that half-mile in a chilly mountain lake just after dawn with over 900 other competitors, and then ride a bike for twelve miles, and run for just over three. The entire experience was a lesson in will power, integrity, accountability, passion, and commitment. Now that I've completed my first triathlon, I'm hooked. That same day I signed up for my next event, this one an "Olympic Distance" triathlon roughly twice as long as my first.

One of the best parts of this first race was watching other competitors begin while I waited my turn to start. To avoid a mid-water pile-up racers began in stages, with elite level, professional athletes starting before the amateur competitors, and finishing long before everyone else. As such, as I waited to begin, I was able to watch some of the best athletes speed through the swim. These competitors were long, lean, specialized athletes who had spent many years honing what was obviously an inborn talent for swimming, biking, and running. Not only were they fast, but they moved with a certain grace that was hard to describe. While I huffed and puffed my way to the finish line, these natural-born athletes made the race look effortless.

Though I strongly believe that anyone can become a fit, fast triathlete, these racers had natural abilities that put their performance beyond the reach of most people, no matter how hard or long they trained. Further, it was obvious that these athletes loved what they were doing. I have seen several races where the elite athletes crossed the finish line with a hard-won expression of sheer bliss stretched across his or her face. There was an energy in the air as the elite athletes arrived. We could tell we were in the presence of something special.

[Some may think these athletes are crazy, and not understand the internal drive that motivates them. The reason some think this, is because their own Soul Purpose does not relate to the Soul Purpose of these athletes. These critics of triathlons undoubtedly have their own "crazy" interests, ambitions, motivations, and passions. By following their bliss, as the triathletes have done, they too can experience the kind of intangible personal rewards, and external success, that these world-class athletes enjoy.]

## WHAT IS SOUL PURPOSE?

That "something special" was the result of what I call "Soul Purpose." In my own coaching and financial advising practice I tell my clients that Soul Purpose is the combination of inborn abilities and passions that identify a person as an individual, and provide a natural direction for that person's most fulfilling life. Soul Purpose is a person's unique psychological fingerprint that defines that person's most powerful strengths, most compelling interests, and most heartfelt passions.

Soul Purpose is most often seen in a person's work. However, Soul Purpose is not something a person does, such as a career. Rather, it is something a person "is." Soul Purpose is expression of self through activities that are simultaneously personally rewarding and contribute to others. Soul Purpose is the pathway to a person's most fulfilling life, because it provides both immediate pleasure and long-term meaning.

The professional athletes at my first triathlon had found an expression of their Soul Purpose. They had discovered their natural, inborn abilities for athletic competition and committed to cultivating these abilities through ongoing education, training and practice. The  external rewards they received were the financial prizes given to top finishers and the paychecks from their sponsors, but even more so the joy of the activity itself. Further, they created significant rewards for others simply by doing what they loved. The racers' sponsors enjoyed more profitable business from the exposure they received. The racers' families got healthier, happier loved ones. And all of the spectators and amateur competitors at the event were inspired by the physical feats they witnessed.

You don't need to be a professional athlete to have a Soul Purpose, however. Everyone has a Soul Purpose. But most people fail to live their Soul Purpose, because they don't believe this way of life is financially viable, or haven't committed to the introspection necessary to identify it.

For those that do identify, commit to, and live their Soul Purpose, the results are incredible. By living Soul Purpose, a person is more productive, wealthier, happier, and more successful than they would be doing anything else.

## SOUL PURPOSE MAXIMIZES PRODUCTIVITY

As part of my triathlon training, I learned to really swim for the first time in my life. Prior to this training, my best attempts at swimming could really be called "energetic floating." When a good friend and I took a transatlantic flight some years ago, he gave me a pair of children's water wings before we boarded the plane, "just in case," he said.

My education in swimming began, as most education does, with theory. I was taught that a swimmer's speed is the result of the number of strokes taken per minute (Stroke Rate) and the distance the swimmer moves with each stroke (Stroke Length). In mathematical terms, the swimmer's Velocity (V) equals Stroke Length (SL) times Stroke Rate (SR).

$$V = SL \times SR$$

A swimmer can go faster by increasing the number of strokes he takes per minute, or by making each stroke propel him farther in the water. These two variables do not contribute equally to a swimmer's speed, however. Stroke Length is responsible for 70% of a swimmer's velocity, while Stroke Rate is responsible for only 30%. That is, the best swimmers in the world focus more on increasing the distance they move with each stroke than they do on paddling faster.

[Having proper form also creates productivity. Knowledge is the difference between activity and productivity.]

To increase Stroke Length, swimmers try to become "slippery," a swimming term that indicates how aerodynamic a swimmer's body is in the water. By being slippery, swimmers reduce the drag of the water on their body. Such swimmers are said to be "fish-like." With less drag, the force of each stroke propels these swimmers farther. Stroke Length is increased by making each stroke more productive.

The body positions that reduce drag on a swimmer can be taught and cultivated through training. But, a small percentage of swimmers just have a natural feel for aerodynamic, fish-like swimming. Swimming is one of the natural abilities that make up these people's Soul Purpose.

Economists use the term "velocity" in much the same way that swimmers do. To economists, Velocity is the productivity of a nation's economy. In mathematical terms, the Velocity (V) of an economy is the Gross Domestic Product (GDP) divided by the Money Supply (MS).

$$V = GDP / MS$$

This mathematical formula compares the value of the goods and services produced in an economy (its "Gross Domestic Product") to the cost of producing those goods and services (the Money Supply).

Velocity can be increased in either of two ways. First, productivity can be increased. This is the economic equivalent of increasing Stroke Length. Second, costs of production can be decreased. This is the economic equivalent of increasing Stroke Rate.

When the lessons of national economies and swimming efficiency are applied to personal finance and happiness, Gross Domestic Product (and Stroke Length) are equivalent to personal productivity, which we'll call "Output." Money Supply (and Stroke Rate) are equivalent to expenses and labor, which we'll call "Input." An individual's Personal Velocity, which measures the value created by a person's work, is Output divided by Input.

**Personal Velocity (PV) = Output / Input**

Therefore, as individuals, to increase the velocity of our work we can either increase its output or decrease its input. The goal is to put continually less time, effort, risk, and money into our work (input) and have it bring continually more productivity and value (output).

The most effective way to achieve this goal is to focus on our strengths. By its very nature, an activity that relies on a strength comes more easily than an activity that relies on an area of weakness. As such, when we work in our strengths, our input is minimized. Expending the same amount of effort, we can produce substantially more value through a strength than someone performing the same work with weak proficiency.

Common sense dictates that work that takes advantage of one's inborn strengths is more productive than work in which one lacks proficiency. However, we live in a society that emphasizes well-roundedness. We are encouraged to address our weaknesses until we have achieved a minimum acceptable proficiency in everything. If we are poor public speakers, we must take a class to overcome this deficiency. If we are bad at math, we are taught that we must study harder, and spend the time necessary to understand it.

Such logic, however well-intentioned, is counter-productive. In the real world, individuals become wealthy, healthy, and happy by focusing on and nurturing whatever it is they already do well. True greatness, as seen in exemplary individuals in all areas of business, sports, the arts, science, academics, research, industry, and all other pursuits, comes from the combination of natural ability and the dedicated development of these skills through a passion for the purpose to which they are applied.

[We have talents that can be cultivated. That's the difference between someone who pursues soul purposes, and someone who views the strengths of others, and is jealous of other's strengths]

## SOUL PURPOSE CREATES GREAT WEALTH

Human Life Value is the ability to create desirable products and services within the marketplace. Human Life Value is composed of an individual's personality, character, talent, skill, knowledge, training, drive, will power, work ethic, ability to articulate, ability to think creatively, and ability to build relationships.

It is our Human Life Value that is used to organize and utilize anything that is tangible and known as property value. In other words, material objects have value only in relation to the Human Life Value that created them and the Human Life

Value that did or will use them. Cell phones and computers were just dirt and metal until people applied their Human Life Value to them. Natural resources have only as much utility as people determine; they only have value as they are used to fulfill people's wants.

Additionally, the products of Human Life Value need not be material. Indeed, anything that anyone finds valuable is the result of someone's Human Life Value. Human Life Value builds skyscrapers and paves highways. But it also writes Grammy-winning songs and inspires church congregations with moving sermons. If a product or service can be bought or sold in the marketplace, it has come from Human Life Value.

An individual's Human Life Value is most efficient when it is used within the realm of one's Soul Purpose. Soul Purpose enables a person's greatest possible wealth, because it gives a competitive advantage in the marketplace. By specializing in the labor that takes advantage of one's inborn abilities and passions, a person is able to create a specific type of value better and more efficiently than anyone else in the world. By creating teams that combine the energies of all members, each working in his or her own Soul Purpose, impossible ambitions are brought within reach.

If a person desires to be wealthy, he should cultivate Human Life Value within the domain of his Soul Purpose. In this way, he understands the proper, highest context of value creation and improves his inborn ability to create value in the marketplace. The natural result of creating such value is wealth.

## SOUL PURPOSE CREATES MEANINGFUL HAPPINESS

Professor Tal Ben-Shahar teaches the most popular class at Harvard University. Every semester, over 900 students enroll in his "Positive Psychology" course, which "focuses on the psychological aspects of a fulfilling and flourishing life." In his book, simply titled Happier, Ben-Shahar writes of the importance of self-determined meaning:

> *"When speaking of a meaningful life, we often talk of having a sense of purpose, but what we sometimes fail to recognize is that finding this sense of purpose entails more than simply setting goals. Having goals or even reaching them does not guarantee that we are leading a purposeful existence. To experience a sense of purpose, the goals we set for ourselves need to be intrinsically meaningful.*

*We could set ourselves the goal of scoring top grades in college or owning a large house, yet still feel empty. To live a meaningful life, we must have a self-generated purpose that possesses personal significance rather than one that is dictated by society's standards and expectations. When we do experience this sense of purpose, we often feel as though we have found our calling. As George Bernard Shaw said, "This is the true joy in life, the being used for a purpose recognized by yourself as a mighty one."*

*Different people find meaning in different things. We may find our calling in starting up a business, working in a homeless shelter, raising children, practicing medicine, or making furniture. The important thing is that we choose our purpose in accordance with our own values and passions rather than conforming to others' expectations. An investment banker who finds meaning and pleasure in her work – who is in it for the right reasons – leads a more spiritual and fulfilling life than a monk who is in his field for the wrong reasons."*

For any given person, Soul Purpose combines the right reasons with the right actions, within the context of that person's life. The natural result is a sense of genuine purpose which inspires passion. This passion is given expression daily, hourly, and every minute through the activities in which that person is engaged.

## SOUL PURPOSE FACILITATES SUCCESS

In his final interview, twentieth-century scholar of mythology Joseph Campbell was asked by Bill Moyers whether he ever had the sense of "being helped by hidden hands." He replied:

*"All the time. It is miraculous. I even have a superstition that has grown on me as a result of invisible hands coming all the time – namely, that if you do follow your bliss you put yourself on a kind of track that has been there all the while, waiting for you, and the life that you ought to be living is the one you are living. When you can see that, you begin to meet people who are in your field of bliss, and they open doors to you. I say, follow your bliss and don't be afraid, and doors will open where you didn't know they were going to be."*

The Universe is governed by timeless, changeless, and irrefutable natural laws, which govern not only the actions and reactions of physical bodies, but the course of mental, psychological, and spiritual events occurring in the Universe. As surely as gravity directs the fall of an apple to the Earth, these other natural laws direct the results that individuals receive from their behaviors.

An individual's Soul Purpose is truly the reason for which that person was born. It is the mission he is on this Earth to perform. The world wants this Soul Purpose desperately. The world demands the value that only that person can create.

When a person's activities are aligned with Universal will, as expressed through Soul Purpose, the Universe acts as a wind at that person's back, assisting with the Purpose to which he has dedicated his life. Seemingly coincidental events, encounters, and meetings occur that advance that person's cause. Such serendipitous occurrences result, as Joseph Campbell says, from a person walking the "track that has been there all the while, waiting for you."

## THE PURPOSE OF THIS BOOK

The remainder of this book is dedicated to portraits of Soul Purpose in action. The reader will be introduced to eleven individuals who have identified, committed to, and now live within their Soul Purpose on a daily basis.

These individuals are to their professions what elite triathletes are to the weekly races they compete in. They are the Michael Jordans of Financial Advising, the Wayne Gretzkys of Productivity Consulting, and the John Elways of Insurance Planning.

[Just as these people are the champions of their sport, this book feastures champions in their industry. They are experts with passion, perspective, and a common foundation of principle. They are a resource for you to live your Soul Purpose, by leveraging theirs.]

By focusing on what they naturally do best, the people portrayed in this book bring substantial value to the marketplace. Additionally, with every day, they become better at the activities in which they already excel. Each day, they cultivate deeper and more powerful Human Life Value within the context of their Soul Purpose.

## THE ACCREDITED NETWORK

The individuals portrayed in this book are members of a distinction and standard called The Accredited Network, formed in 2004 with the specific objective of supporting Soul Purpose among its members. The Accredited Network is a group of like-minded yet diverse individuals committed to creating substantial value for their clients, business partners, and personal associates by leveraging the Soul Purposes of all other members of The Accredited Network. They are expert advisors with a depth of knowledge, ability, and insight in a particular area related to their Soul Purpose.

[They turn philosophy into personal prosperity for you.]

To accomplish the ambitious objective of The Accredited Network, members declare and elaborate the unique value they offer in the marketplace through their Soul Purpose. Whenever other members of The Accredited Network identify a client, colleague, or personal associate in search of such value, this person is referred to The Accredited Network member who can fulfill that search.

Members of The Accredited Network have access to unique, invitation-only events such as the recent Training Seminar in which Garrett White, one of the featured entrepreneurs in this book, taught members and clients of The Accredited Network how to use their own Soul Purpose to further wealth, joy and ultimately their own spirituality.

## RECEIVING VALUE FROM THIS BOOK

More than anything, this book is intended to provide value to its readers. Readers can receive value from this book in many ways:

By understanding and incorporating the examples of Soul Purpose in this book into your own life, you can begin to identify and live your own Soul Purpose. Each of the eleven people profiled herein followed his or her own path to Soul Purpose. Likely, one of these paths will resemble your own journey to finding that combination of inborn ability and passions that truly inspires you.

Next, the services of each of the individuals profiled in this book are available within the greater marketplace. Contact information is provided for each person, so that readers might take advantage of the products and services that each of these people offer. Many of these individuals take part in mentoring or coaching programs that make their expertise in the realm of Soul Purpose available to others seeking their own path to their ideal life. Feel free to contact these people to learn how they might create value for you. One of the easiest ways to begin is by filling out the card included in this book.

Readers of this book are also invited to investigate membership in The Accredited Network. As a member, you will have the support of a highly educated, highly motivated, and highly enlightened group of like-minded entrepreneurs, each with unique expertise, principles, and passions.

Membership in The Accredited Network is divided into tiers, each of which provides additional benefits and entails additional responsibilities. The first membership tier of The Accredited Network is open to all members of the public. All membership tiers thereafter require prospective applicants to fulfill specific requirements for advancement. These requirements ensure that members at these tiers are able to create greater and greater value for their colleagues in The Accredited Network.

# CHAPTER 1

# GARRETT B. GUNDERSON
### The Freedom FastTrack, LLC.

*Garrett B Gunderson is a natural-born entrepreneur who began his first officially licensed business by the age of 15 and immediately began to win business competitions across the state of Utah. Garrett took state for entrepreneurship in high school, and by the age of 18 was named the SBA Young Entrepreneur of the Year in a statewide competition for business owners under the age of 30.*

*Garrett first began focusing his abundant energy and talent on the financial services industry while attending Southern Utah University. He entered the industry by 19 and became an advisor to several of his professors. Garrett is the youngest member to ever be on the Alumni Board for the University. Garrett was active in Sigma Chi where he earned the Constantine and Balfour distinctions—the two highest honors given by the fraternity. Garrett served as a senator for the school of business and was President of the United Greek Council. He was also honored multiple years as one of the top five male contributors and was the youngest person ever to be inducted into The Old Main Society for his philanthropy and service to the University.*

*Garrett began making a six-figure income his first year out of college, and was a millionaire by age 26. He is now the founder, partner or executive of 5 successful companies. Garrett's passion for helping others break down barriers to become successful is most evident in The Freedom FastTrack—a unique process he authored and designed to help others recognize potential, which can then be transformed into production through value creation. Garrett is also the author of the highly acclaimed book Killing Sacred Cows.*

*Garrett is married to his best friend, Carrie. They have two wonderful sons, Breck and Roman, who are the light of Garrett's life and the permission to be silly and fun. He attributes his success to a hunger for learning and finding the greatest teachers, learning from them, teaching others in turn, and thereby developing amazing relationships. He also acknowledges that as his spirituality has strengthened so have his relationships and ideas.*

## A MILK CARTON HOUSE

When I was in kindergarten my class built some little houses out of milk cartons. I put a lot of effort into mine and I thought it was the most amazing, incredible, creative thing that anyone had ever come up with. I was so proud of that milk carton house, and I couldn't wait to take it home and show my mom how great it was. However, my teacher had a different idea. At the end of the day she collected all of them. She put them all up on this high shelf where we couldn't reach them. Then she said to us, "If you want your house back then you have to memorize the street number that is on your real house." So even though it was freezing cold in the winter I would go outside of my house every morning before school and stare at those three numbers 3-6-7, over and over. Then later at school I would stand in line for my turn to say the numbers that would get me my milk carton house back. But when it was my turn I kept messing up. This went on for days. I'd say 6-3-7 or 7-6-3, et cetera, but I just couldn't ever quite remember the right order when it was my turn.

Eventually my milk carton house was the very last one left. Everyone else had already memorized their correct house numbers and had gotten to take their milk carton house home. I wanted to have my milk carton house back so much. My teacher told me I had one last chance to get it right. I was so nervous. I tried so hard to remember those numbers in order, but I got it wrong...again. Then she threw away my milk carton house that I was so proud of. It was gone. All my efforts didn't amount to anything. I was humiliated. I had lost. There I was, five years old, and in that moment I decided that I must be stupid. I didn't want anyone else to know how stupid I was. In fact, I spent nearly the next two decades of my life attempting to prove to myself, and to everyone else, that I wasn't stupid, and it was all because of three numbers and a milk carton. We'll come back to this story later.

## A GLIMPSE OF SOUL PURPOSE

If you're Mozart and composing beautiful classical music at the age of five then you're probably not going to have a difficult time discovering your Soul Purpose. But for most of us Soul Purpose is not always so apparent. Discovering our talents and passions is often a journey, and that is certainly my story. I started my first business in the small mining town I grew up in. I was fifteen years old. It was a physical business of washing and cleaning cars involving a lot of hard, tedious labor. There was this particularly warm day where I had my shirt off, sweating up a storm. I had been working for several long, hot hours. The vehicle I was cleaning had gotten repossessed in Mexico and it was filthy. Imagine the dirtiest car you've ever seen and multiply that vision by ten! After working on it for over eight hours, it still wasn't even close to being done. Three of those hours were spent just getting all the garbage out of the vehicle. I had to takeout out the seats just to get at some of the trash, which had gotten into places you wouldn't think possible. It was sticky, gross and in every way disgusting. But I have always been someone who wants to do a good job or not at all, so I kept going. The sun had already gone down when the realization struck that "this isn't what I want to do for the rest of my life."

However, I did discover that I was exceptionally good at certain things. I found that even though I didn't want to wash all those dirty cars all by myself, I enjoyed many aspects of my first business. I started hiring employees. What I learned throughout the next few years, was that I really loved owning and running my own business. I enjoyed selling the services, coming up with creative ideas to attract more clients. I loved coming up with personal touches, such as having garbage bags, air fresheners, and customer coupons customized with my company's log and offering premier detailing services. I got satisfaction out of making sure a great job was done, and that the clients were happy. In fact, I loved almost everything about it—except for the actual washing the vehicle part. On the other hand, there are plenty of people who prefer manual labor to running a business. They wouldn't enjoy marketing services, or having the ultimate responsibility for seeing that a job got done the right way, whereas that's the part that I got the most energy from.

While running my business, I ended up winning a competition called the Rural Young Entrepreneur and was awarded five hundred dollars for planning a presentation and speaking about my business. I found the experience to be exhilarating, and I thought about how many cars I would have had to wash to make that same amount of money. I also realized that working is not about activity it's about productivity. It was an early glimpse of the concept of Soul Purpose when I started to realize that people could do what they enjoyed, provide a valuable service and make money while doing it. But back when I was still washing vehicles well into the dark, I only had one small piece of the puzzle.

## AN INJURY & AN OPPORTUNITY

Also back in high school while I was still running my business, I was a decent baseball player. I was a pitcher with a great record, on a great team. I was having a great time. Then something seemingly horrible happened. I blew out my knee, and I didn't get to be on the team my senior year. But here's how things turned out; even though I didn't get to play sports to the level that I wanted to, I was the only state champion from my school that year. I ended up taking the state championship title in business. I won The Governor's Entrepreneur of the Year, got a $5,000 prize and I discovered some interesting things about myself. For example, I came to further realize that I had an innate talent for public speaking. I overcame the fear of speaking in public when I was given the opportunity to speak to very high-level, influential business people all over the state. The governor personally awarded me that prize, and some truly amazing opportunities came out of it.

So how does this all tie together? When I blew out my knee, I was really disappointed. But, I also knew that everything happens for a reason. I realized that I didn't get to choose to go back in time and not blow out my knee and play ball my senior year, but I did get to choose where I went from that moment forward. I could either dwell on my perceived defeat, or I could rise up to a new challenge. Rather than whining, sulking and feeling sorry for myself, I chose to take my business to an extraordinary new level, because I had that extra time to devote to it that would have been taken up by baseball. All the while, my business kept on running while my knee was injured because I had a good team of employees. I ended up getting a university scholarship out of the experience, while making great connections and wonderful friends.

I'm still doing business with people I met during that time in my life. I was able to impact a lot of lives and was impacted by others as well. Was I sad that I blew my knee out? Of course I was. But I made the best of it and things turned out for the best. Figuratively speaking, I still have my knee blown out on a regular basis, in situations where things don't turn out the way I would hope. But I remember that with every "injury" comes an opportunity.

## CHOOSING THE PATH

When I graduated from college I had a very difficult decision. For everyone else, these particular decisions seemed incredibly wonderful, but for me it seemed overwhelming at times. I had 11 top-notch companies trying to recruit me to work for their firm. They were all offering me what most would consider amazing jobs that college grads don't usually get to walk into. I would talk to my professors and they would say to go with a particularly prestigious firm, because not only would it be good for me, but it would bring prestige to the university to have a new grad recruited into such a respected company. In fact, for several positions it would be a first for the university to have a student recruited to work for such a high-level firm. My family was saying what jobs they thought sounded best, and my friends had their opinions too. Based on the decision I made, I would be moving to New York, Milwaukee or a number of other far off places. The opportunities were amazing. I knew it would seem really stupid if I turned them all down, and as you know from the milk carton disaster at the beginning of this chapter—having people think I was stupid was my worst fear. But in my gut, none of it felt right.

I wanted to live in Utah and stay close to the people I knew and loved. I wanted to work according to principles that I knew to be true, rather than according to popular opinion, or someone else's mandates. But it was a really hard decision. I could have a great, seemingly guaranteed income with an established company, or I could do what my heart was telling me to do. I was paralyzed with fear for some time, which started to get me down. At times, I would stay in my bed in the morning for hours thinking about what I was going to do.

It was my last semester of college, what should have been one of the most exciting times of my life, and yet I was feeling worried and anxious about my impending decision. I knew that ultimately I had two choices, I could do what I really wanted to do, or do the so-called "smart" thing. I knew if I forged the path I felt was right for me, then it would all rely on me. I wasn't sure if I was strong enough, if I had enough clients, if I could ultimately be successful doing what I loved to do. If I went to work for a large, prestigious firm, I would be okay, but I would be missing out on part of my own personal Soul Purpose, which happens to be connecting people, creating a vision, articulating complex situations easily, and forming models for production, which were all things I could better do in the context of running my own business. I didn't consciously understand the concept of Soul Purpose at the time, but I had a pretty strong feeling that I could either do what I wanted to do, or I could do what others wanted me to do. I chose to follow my own path.

When I talked to the Dean of my school he gave me just that little nudge of encouragement that I needed. Unlike everyone else who was thinking only of the traditional definition of security and prestige, he pointed out my personal productivity. He pointed out the fact that I was already making more than he was. I was only working as a financial advisor part-time since I was still in school. In light of that fact, and considering my attributes as an individual, he assured me that I was going to do just fine on my own, and that I didn't need to take a job that wasn't right for me. I already knew it, but sometimes that little voice of confirmation can make a world of difference when you're hearing so many conflicting arguments. I took that encouragement and ran with it.

I went on to create my own successful financial advising firm, which has evolved to include mentoring and advising in not just the financial realm of life, but in every other important aspect of life as well. It was only then that I fully realized my own personal Soul Purpose, which was to help others live their own Soul Purpose. I knew that I wanted to do more than help people become rich. I also wanted to help them become more productive, more spiritual, happier, and to live their ideal lives as the very best version of who they were meant to be. Money alone doesn't bring joy and success into one's life. However, having financial freedom is usually a prerequisite to finding freedom in other areas of life, so that's what I started with.

People who are bogged down with worries about their financial situation, are usually not in the right state of mind to create breakthroughs in other areas of their life—whether they are the poorest of the poor, or the richest of the rich. We are now advising the very best and brightest individuals and corporations all across the nation. We're successful because the principle based strategies and systems that we offer deal with the Human Life Value of each individual, therefore they work so much more effectively than "conventional" financial strategies. Financial success isn't about strategies, it's a byproduct of who you are. We began helping individuals realize that they were their own best products and were there own "guaranteed" financial success. We show people how to invest in accordance with their Soul Purpose, so that they are no longer gambling but actually investing in something that they believe in and have control over. We instruct business owners, CEOs and upper-management on how to more effectively synergize their Soul Purpose with the Soul Purpose of their team members, and many other incredible training programs through the Curriculum for Wealth and the Freedom FastTrack programs, which are now licensed to other advisors throughout the nation. None of this would have been possible if I would have gone with the safe bet, instead of with what I knew I was brought into this world to do. I further came to know that the only risky thing in finances is to not live your Soul Purpose. It can be a paradox at times, because in the short-run, such as in the situation where I considered taking a job with an established firm, it can seem like a choice where you can have security or Soul Purpose. But what I discovered was that living Soul Purpose is the ultimate security and the best measure of genuine success, rather than the false sense and definition of security taught by society.

## AN AHA MOMENT

But before all these incredible things happened, I still had some important lessons to learn. When I first got married I was still stuck in the Consumer Condition, which is a state were an individual, or society as a whole, is not living in Soul Purpose, but rather buying in to falsehoods that keep us from contributing more than we consume. I grew up in an area full of wonderful people, but who unfortunately were living in the Consumer Condition and I thought that was just the way things were. I was making plenty of money but I had this idea that I should save every penny, accumulate net worth and that would be the ticket to success. I bought into the concept of wanting really padded investments and savings accounts. I owned over a dozen real estate properties pretty much right out of college, but I told my wife we couldn't have our own house until we had even more money. I bought into a common fallacy.

I thought you had to sacrifice in order to have your dreams. So, I was fully prepared to keep sacrificing indefinitely, and furthermore; I was going to have my wife sacrifice what she wanted as well. When we went on a vacation, for example, instead of allowing my wife and I to truly enjoy ourselves, I made a point to scrimp and save in every way I could think of, which didn't turn out to make the vacation all that fun. I didn't realize it at the time, but my distorted concept of success was affecting my relationship with my wife and everyone else. I had created a prison, but I didn't even see it. I thought, "I'm happy, she's happy. She's got a good life." But I couldn't see how I was actually damaging our relationship and causing unnecessary conflicts over money.

I was deferring my life into the future because I thought that my personal value was tied to the amount of money I had at that given moment, even though in reality it never was and never will be. However, at the time, I thought savings were going to be better than investing in my ability to produce. What I found out later was the exact opposite. You pursue your dreams precisely so that you can live in the moment, rather than to live in the scarcity paradigm, constantly worried about savings and going without.

Things started to change after I went to a seminar led by Ron Zeller, who now happens to be a business partner of mine. During this seminar I recognized that I had this huge blind spot that I couldn't see in regards to money, and in regards to many other areas of my life as well. Where did this blind spot come from? I realized that it stemmed partially from that milk carton house experience I had as a child that convinced me that I must be stupid. I was trying to prove to the world that I wasn't stupid by having lots of money. It didn't really make much sense though, because my wife and I had money, but we were living like paupers in an apartment complex and driving around this car we didn't like. My wife was wearing clothes that she didn't want to wear, because I didn't want her to buy new clothes, even though we could afford it. In fact, her mother was buying clothes for her on her teacher's salary, because I was too worried about saving money to buy her new clothes.

In short, I made sure we sacrificed in every area for no good reason. I was simply trying to prove to everyone that I was really smart, and that's how society tradition- ally teaches people to be "smart", by "wisely" hoarding their money. I was making a 6-figure income, which was a lot more than the other couples in our apartment complex, but it wouldn't have mattered how much money we did, or didn't, have because I was still living in the poverty paradigm at that point. I was in scarcity. It was impacting nearly every area of my life but I didn't even recognize it, because I was too busy comparing myself to everyone else.

Compared to other people our age, we were living a pretty good life, so it never dawned on me how far into the Consumer Condition I was living. I was judging myself by how much money I was saving, and I was also judging others for spending their money rather than saving it. It was a form of pride and arrogance, but I thought I was being humble by living below my means rather than focusing on my means, and expanding them. I got caught up in being right and in showing everyone how great I was. I wasn't loving my life, in fact I wasn't really even living my life. I was trying to live up to an idea that didn't even exist. I was letting an impression made on me when I was 5 years old determine how I lived my life.

I was 24 years old when I realized this at that seminar, and from that moment on I started living my life. That paradigm shift took one second, but once I realize it—everything changed. I called my wife and told her my realization; that I was delaying our lives for no good reason. We talked, and in 45 minutes our relationship was completely transformed. She completely forgave me for my selfishness. We started experiencing the life that we actually wanted. She got into her dream home, got to wear the clothes she wanted, we started going places and doing things without constantly scrimping. Here's the best part, I started having more success, and making more money living this way than I ever had before while living in a scarcity mindset and saving every penny.

It's not like we started living outside of our means. We just started "living" and the means kept increasing. I would never advocate that someone start being irresponsible with their money, and just hope that things work out. Personally, I'm a great steward with my money, and the few times I haven't been, I've learned immensely from the experience. However, I was able to realize that money has no intrinsic value. If you're not using money to live a wonderful life and to help others live a wonderful life, then what use is it sitting in a bank account or investment portfolio? I view the whole world differently because I invest in my Soul Purpose, which allows me to be the best producer possible, and to live in abundance rather than scarcity. Most importantly, I am able to see though a whole new paradigm that allows me to enjoy the moments. Now I focus on making course corrections to help me stay as balanced as possible. Whereas when I was completely out of balance, I had to deal with "forced corrections', which is inevitably painful. My life is now in a state of growth and progression, whereas it used to be in a state of scarcity and frustration. It all started with that simple realization.

## OVERCOMING CHALLENGES

My biggest challenge to overcome was to stop looking around at everyone else, but rather to create my own standard for what I wanted out of life. For example, I might look at someone in misery and compare myself to them. Comparatively, I have a great life, but is it really the life I want? Is it ideal? I was complacent based on limiting social beliefs that weren't even true, but at the time I bought into it. These limiting factors exist all over the world. In fact, many of us at some point believe things to be true that actually turn out to be very false, but we're not willing to confront it. There are many different reasons for this.

Some of us enjoy having a false security, or are too comfortable with a lie to give it up for the truth. For me it was a fear of how other's would judge me if I starting conforming to my own standard rather than theirs. Because I was worried that some- one might think I was stupid. But as soon as I was willing to give up how I "looked" and actually started looking instead, a whole new world opened up to me. I started being honest with myself, and what I came to realize was that most people in the world don't want to know the truth—they're frightened by it actually —just like I was. This is because when we look at truth we're forced to confront our own "Sacred Cows", which are ideas or beliefs that are, for one reason or another, unreasonably immune to criticism.

A lot of these false, limiting beliefs as they pertain to the financial realm are covered in my book Killing Sacred Cows. By the term killing sacred cows, I'm referring to exposing the limiting myths, fallacies, and misguided traditions about the world of personal finance, but this also applies to every realm of our life. This kind of revolutionary understanding naturally creates greater opportunity, happiness and wealth for mission-driven individuals. By the term mission-driven I am, of course, referring to people who live their Soul Purpose. I'm referring to those individuals who choose to stop deferring their lives into an unknown future, and are ready to start living their ideal life in the now. When I finally got to the point that I could confront my own "Sacred Cows", things really started to change.

## WHY DOESN'T EVERYONE LIVE HIS OR HER SOUL PURPOSE?

Through living my Soul Purpose and giving up the Consumer Condition, I began living a much fuller, richer and more satisfying life. I have seen this same transformation take place with so many of our clients. So, if Soul Purpose is as wonderful as those who are living it claim, then why aren't more people living their Soul Purpose? There are three main reasons why people don't live their Soul Purpose. The biggest reason is because many people aren't even aware that the concept exists. The majority of the planet is entrenched in the Consumer Condition, and most people don't ever truly realize that they could do what they love to do and be successful. Secondly, once people understand the concept, they don't always understand how to go about actualizing it. Lastly, even if they know their Soul Purpose and the right path, if they don't have the right support structure then fear can override their intentions.

Another aspect of why some people don't know how to live their Soul Purpose, is that many individuals don't have a developed sense of who they are in the first place. Even though they were born with a valuable and unique set of traits and talents, they may not have chosen, or have been able to, cultivate their individual gifts. Being born into a situation where you were not loved or valued, for example, can make this journey much more difficult for some. But I believe it is ultimately each person's individual responsibility to discover and live their own Soul Purpose. For most of us, it isn't something that just falls into our lap and manifests itself without any previous thought or effort. Breakthroughs can happen in a moment, but only if the individual is prepared and willing to see it for what it is. When our minds are weighed down with limiting beliefs, truth can hit us in the face and we won't recognize it. Some people may even believe that they are living their Soul Purpose because they are very good at what they do. But the truth is, you can be very good at something and not enjoy it. That is because it may be a type of work that utilizes some of your talents, but not your passion. For example, you could be an excellent attorney and win every case, but if it doesn't cultivate and provide you with "renewable" energy that leads to an inspired passion, then chances are—it's not your Soul Purpose…it's just something you happen to be good at. There is a difference.

## FINDING SOUL PURPOSE

It can be a lifelong journey for some. I helped develop The Freedom FastTrack programs to save people years of wasted time and energy. The Freedom FastTrack specializes in helping individuals realize their Soul Purpose and then quickly transform one's Soul Purpose into actual value in the marketplace. But there are some things you can do to get the process started. I suggest asking your friends and family what they believe is great about you, and what characteristics and attributes they have noticed to be consistent in your life. I developed the Producer Power Hour™ system (producerpowerhour.com) specifically to help individuals identify, develop and live their Soul Purpose on a daily basis. I've spent a lot of money in my life on programs, seminars, and other educational programs, but it wouldn't get me anywhere if I didn't understand how to integrate that information into my daily life. The thing is, most of us don't usually have an ideal support structure, along with incredible mentors encouraging us to live to our fullest potential on a daily basis. So I developed the Producer Power system to do just that. It brings the best minds on the planet together to instruct, uplift and edify Producer Power Hour members on a daily basis through a variety of systems. Basically, it allows people to go within, so they never have to go without. For myself, the Producer Power Hour has proven to be the most powerful system that anyone can tap into on a daily basis to experience extraordinary transformation. Without the Producer Power Hour, it becomes tempting to wait for opportunity to "happen" or "come along", but Producer Power Hour participants develop the ability to consistently create their own opportunities.

I have found that anyone who takes this transformative opportunity seriously will inevitably begin to see powerful transformations in their lives. The Producer Power Hour is a wonderful way for individuals to rid themselves of a scarcity mindset on a consistent basis, so they can always live in abundance and more fully understand and live their Soul Purpose.

Overall, it's a system to create the most favorable conditions for individuals to live a life that they love. It is also a support structure, a mindset, a philosophy and more. But on a the most basic level, the Producer Power Hour is an individualized daily routine consisting of "ten minutes of transformation" in every major track of life including the financial realm, the spiritual realm, the mental realm, the physical realm, and the social realm. For anyone wanting to identify, enhance or further develop his or her individual Soul Purpose, I would recommend the Producer Power Hour as a wonderful place to start. Ultimately, you'll be responsible for discovering, developing and implementing your own individual Soul Purpose in life, but a little guidance can certainly go a long ways. (If you'd like to try out this system for a month at no charge, sign up at producerpowerhour.com, and use the code EconSP)

As it turns out, the Dean at my university was someone who gave me some pretty good guidance, and it ended up benefiting the university as well. I've donated more to Southern Utah University than anyone else under 30, and became the youngest member of the Old Main Society. I've sponsored huge bands like the Goo-Goo Dolls to go and play at the university, I've been a guest speaker, I've hired students to work at my firm, and I've basically found a lot of ways to give back. None of that would have been possible if I hadn't believed my college Dean's good advice to follow my dreams and be true to who I am. Now I own firms centered around doing the same things for others, but in a much more powerful way. The Producer Power Hour is the daily support structure, while The Freedom FastTrack consists of highly specialized, intensive programs to allow individuals to reach the really big goals in life. Not only do all of these programs encourage individuals to live their dreams, but even more importantly, they provide tangible, comprehensive systems for doing so that are easy to understand and implement. The Freedom FastTrack provides a path to success that is repeatable, efficient, highly productive and virtually fail-proof. Helping others find their Soul Purpose is what I always wanted to do, and to be a part of. Now I am actually doing it. It's incredible where following your own Soul Purpose can lead you.

## SOUL PURPOSE SECURITY

However, there was a time in my life, as I mentioned earlier, that I was terrified of living my Soul Purpose. I thought it was going to be risky, and that I might not succeed. What I have found out since then is that there is, in actuality, nothing in the world more secure than living your Soul Purpose. How could being the very best version of who you really are, be risky? Who in the world can be better at your God-given talents in just the right combination that you have? No one! Your Soul Purpose is unique, and that is what makes you infinitely valuable to the world. You have something to offer than no one else has. It's become a cliché to say that everyone has a special gift, but everyone does have a unique combination of special gifts and talents. Each individual truly does have his or her own unique purpose for being on the Earth, along with a set of complimentary talents that can facilitate that purpose. Once that truth is realized, people have the innate power to transform their lives. They come to realize that the riskiest thing you could ever do is to not follow your Soul Purpose.

Unfortunately, most people don't understand the concept. Many people are so caught up in the Consumer Condition that they will never break free to become whom they truly want to be—whom they were truly meant to be. That ignorance is the true source of every pain, trial and hardship on this planet. For some of us, it's hard then easy versus easy then hard. If you always stick to the perceived "safe route" through life, chances are you'll end up with less security, less joy and less abundance. Using myself as an example, I could have easily taken the "safe job". Initially, at least, it would have been easier to work for an established firm and get my check every month, rather than to start up my own business, which required me to have faith in myself, my talents and abilities. The reality is that honoring your Soul Purpose does sometimes require tough choices and hard work up front, but the end result is always worth it. My life is now "easier" than it would have been relying on a paycheck, especially because I'm doing what I'm passionate about. I'm doing what I would want to do, even if I wasn't getting paid for it. What could be "easier" than that?

Even so, just like I was once afraid to live my Soul Purpose, many other people have shared with me that they have also lived consciously, or perhaps subconsciously, thinking that they weren't good enough, weren't smart enough, weren't valuable enough. This may seem strange, but when I had that breakthrough moment at that seminar and realized that I wasn't stupid, I stopped worrying about net worth, and about saving every last dollar. Within a few weeks my wife was in her dream home. We actually started doing more business because of it. I suddenly had a different confidence. I felt comfortable having people come to my house for meetings. We entertain more, which I love to do. I love throwing get-togethers and parties. I am a "connector" in business and in my personal life. That's who I am, but we couldn't do that in our small apartment. Basically, I started having material things be an expression of who I am, rather than an expression of what I was afraid of.

Once that happens for you, you will find no greater security in life than in living your Soul Purpose. This growth became exponential for me when I started purposefully meditating, cultivating my energy, protecting my health and studying to become more knowledgeable in my field each morning. I wanted to share that expansive experience with others to help them enhance and maximize their ability to live their Soul Purpose, which is why I created the Producer Power Hour. As with the Freedom FastTrack programs, the purpose is to take an individual or corporation to a new level in a just a few months that many strive for their whole lives without ever attaining. It's like taking a jet plane from New York to LA instead of walking it. You may get to the same point eventually, but think of the wasted time, pain and energy. It's an incredible thing for my clients when they realize that their investment in their own education and progression has given them the best return on investment of their lives. You have to Be, before you Do, before you Have. This Be > Do > Have phenomenon is easily understood, but hard to put into practice. Without a practical, efficient outline and reproducible system to utilize, most people fail to realize their full potential. Each of us already has this transformational power within, but both the Producer Power Hour and The Freedom FastTrack programs simply facilitate developing and utilizing that power in an efficient, powerful way to accomplish the things that you were always meant to do.

## INVESTING IN SOUL PURPOSE

Since experiencing these major paradigm shifts, I now invest in things that help me increase my Soul Purpose. I don't look at investments in terms of products. I also don't look at money's value in terms of net worth and savings accounts. I look at what allows me to enjoy life to the fullest, and to be the most productive person possible. I now understand that my education and my mindset is the absolute most important thing I could ever invest in. It has offered me the very best return on investment that I could ever possibly make, because it's what allows me to be more productive and continue to live life to the fullest in every sense. I'm constantly reading and going to events, and engaging in things that bring my mind to a higher level of awareness. I chose to live NOW how people say they want to live when they retire. I do what I want to do, and I have the things that I want to have.

However, I do not believe that having "things" is what creates value in life. I drive luxury cars, but they're just nice cars that I enjoy driving—it doesn't define me as a person. I have a beautiful home. I own expensive, beautiful art. I have an incredible new building specified to create an ultimate experience for my clients. These things don't define me, they are simply some of the fruits of my labor. I'm no longer trapped in a mindset where I feel compelled to hoard my money to enjoy in 30 years. I'm living my life now, and by doing so I am creating more wealth and happiness in my life and in the lives of others than ever before. I'm not waiting to do the things that I want to do now. In fact, I'm so passionate about what I do that sometimes it's hard for me to go to sleep! I love engaging in my Soul Purpose and producing value for myself and for others. It gives me energy and brings me joy.

Why did I ever "wait" to start experiencing that? Because, I listened to this good intentioned but false advice: "If you'll sacrifice now, you'll have it really good in the future." That sounded so reasonable and rung true to me at first. I bought into it. I couldn't see how poisonous that philosophy can become. I was looking forward to "someday" rather than actually enjoying my life and living in the present. Now I understand that someday is today. I ask myself, "What today would give me the most fulfilling life, the most joy and the most happiness?" If I were to always wait for someday, where would I be today? Not where I want to be, that much is certain. As soon as we say "someday" we start getting into trouble.

## THE DANGER OF A DEFERRED LIFE

You might be thinking, "But patience is a virtue. You can't just do exactly what you want today and not plan for tomorrow." In some contexts that is perfectly true. But if you're deferring your life using "someday" as an excuse, you'll never get where you want to be TODAY. Let me give you an example from my own life. I used to do it with eating. I keep pretty fit these days, but I used to play the "someday" game with food. I would think, "I really ought to start eating better." Then I would think to myself, "I'll start on Monday." Since I was going to start eating healthy on Monday, I felt that in the meantime I may as well eat whatever I wanted, which meant I was basically going to pig out on junk food. Guess what happened? I started gaining a lot of weight. This is a specific example, but I can truly say that anytime I see people trying to defer anything in life, regardless of the situation, it does not work out for them the way they want it to.

Don't buy into the idea of deferring your ideal life, of deferring happiness, of deferring doing what you love. The mindset of deferred happiness is part of the Consumer Condition of scarcity, which becomes a self-fulfilling prophecy. If you're always waiting for something to be "enough"—there will never be enough. It's that simple. What I learned from the unfortunate experience of choosing to live unnecessarily in the Consumer Condition back when my wife and I first got married is this: you can never get back the memories that you chose to not have! I could have given my wife her dream home sooner. I could have made our vacations and activities so much more enjoyable, but I chose to live in a scarcity mindset and deny both of us that experience even though we could have easily afforded it. Once I understood that someday is today, we started having so much more abundance, happiness and harmony than we had ever previously experienced.

## LEVERAGING SOUL PURPOSE

My biggest desire has always been to create something that would allow people who would traditionally be considered "ordinary" to perform extraordinary. My whole life I had this innate desire to elevate everyone I come in contact with. I wanted people to be able to see their potential. Even though it wasn't my original intent, I found that by elevating others and leveraging their Soul Purpose, I was also able to accomplish so much more myself. I was able to do more of what I loved because I was helping others to do more of what they loved. Soul Purpose has an incredible, synergistic effect on others. When you start truly being YOU and honoring your own Soul Purpose, you are also giving others permission to more fully be themselves and to live their own Soul Purposes.

It's incredible how it works in such a complementary fashion, and yet so many of us don't take full advantage of it. Through living my Soul Purpose I became more prosperous and was able to give my friends and family greater opportunities, as well. Some of them even work for me now in areas where they naturally excel and are drawn to. People have told me, "Don't do business with family and friends." But what I have found to be true is that if you're doing the right thing, then you can do business with whoever else is also doing the right thing, regardless of who that person is.

I don't live in fear, or with secrets. My life is an open book. I don't hide anything, because I'm not ashamed of who I am, and I have nothing to hide. At my firm, for example, anyone can see the books that want to see the books. There are no secrets about who's doing what and who's making what amount of money from what they're doing. That's one of the many benefits of living Soul Purpose, and having a team that also lives Soul Purpose. I'm not saying every firm has to be just like mine, but the point is that people who are living their Soul Purpose move beyond competition, it's about being who you are, doing what you're good at doing and allowing everyone to mutually benefit.

I practice this same openness in my blog (www.GarrettBGunderson.com), in books I write, my radio broadcasts and in the events that I host. I'm not afraid anymore to let others know who I really am. If I'm struggling with something, I'll let you know that too. But now instead of dwelling on a problem or setback for weeks at a time, I quickly find a solution—sometimes in only a few seconds—and get on with living the life that I love. Most importantly, I try to share my breakthroughs with others. I'm completely committed to helping people discover and live their potential, which makes them happier, more productive and wealthier.

Back when I was still in a scarcity mindset, I would think about how much I was paying my assistant, for example, and think, "I could go buy a Rolex with that money". Living in that kind of a scarcity mindset causes all kinds of unnecessary pain and irritations on a daily basis. What I didn't understand then, but what I clearly understand now, is that people—not things—are the true assets.

Now that I more fully understand and live my Soul Purpose I love giving, and the more I give the more I receive. I love to give and receive knowledge. I love to educate and be educated. Sharing concepts with others that I know will enrich and improve their lives, is an energizing and rewarding experience for me. The Accredited Network is the perfect expression of this. By bringing together a network of talented experts in their own fields, we are able to leverage and support each other's Soul Purposes. As I live my Soul Purpose, I am able to energize and enrich others, as well. That is the true beauty of living Soul Purpose. You will have and give more abundantly than you ever could in doing something that is not in line with your Soul Purpose.

The Accredited Network is a wonderful example of Soul Purpose in action. They're able to serve others far beyond offering general financial advice, because everyone is specializing in exactly what they're good at, but all are working together for the same objective of increasing the client's prosperity. Often your average financial advice is laced with well-intentioned but misleading or contradictory information, because most financial advisors do not understand the subtle lies and money myths that pervade society. They are trapped in the Consumer Condition themselves, so they can hardly empower their clients to break free.

Some people may misunderstand Soul Purpose to be a selfish thing. When it is really the opposite. Living your Soul Purpose is the greatest gift you could ever give the world. Some people may think from a false sense of duty that there is virtue in doing something that makes one miserable, or in being poor, but the truth is that they are not only doing themselves a disservice, but also everyone they come in contact with. They are depriving the world of their unique talents and attributes because they are not utilizing them for everyone's greatest benefit. Unfortunately, they are also depriving themselves and their loved ones of living the fullest, most joyful and rewarding lives that they could ever imagine.

## THE PRODUCER PARADIGM

When I was 10 years old in school, I remember thinking that it was ironic that the kids who were always getting sent to "de"tention were actually the ones getting all of the "at"tention. I thought about how unfortunate it was that these kids who weren't at all interested in learning, and weren't letting other students learn either, were the one's taking up all of the teacher's energy. Later I was going camping with my father when he pulled off to the side of the road and started picking up garbage. I said, "Hey, what are we doing, why are we picking up other people's garbage for them?" He said, "Look, I don't care who made the mess, I'm concerned about making any community I'm around better because I live there, not making it worse." I thought back to the detention phenomena and about what my dad was saying, and I knew what he was saying was right. I committed to myself at that moment that I was going to be someone that always created more value than I consumed. I decided that I was going to take personal responsibility for making my community great, rather than to just leaving it up to others.

Each of us has that same opportunity to create more than we take, and find greater joy in being a Producer (one who produces more than they consume) than we ever could as a Consumer (one who consumes more than they produce). Whether you're running your own business or working for someone else, it doesn't matter so long as you're living your Soul Purpose. When we live our Soul Purpose, we're creating value. Enjoying the experience of creating value is the most natural thing on Earth. It's what we want to do, what we love to do and what we would ultimately do even if money were of no concern. Retirement becomes irrelevant when you're already doing what you love. You could technically retire, but if you were truly living your Soul Purpose, you'd just want to keep doing what you were already doing, because that is what brings you the most joy, the most energy, and the very most rewarding life possible.

You'll understand your Soul Purpose when you can answer this question: what would you do all day long whether or not you got paid to do it? When you actually find a way to answer that in a way that is deliverable as value to others, then you will be living Soul Purpose. Not only will you get to do what you love, but you'll get paid for it, and you'll be very successful. You'll be doing something that only you can do to that level, which makes your services and products valuable indeed.

## SOUL PURPOSE BREAKTHROUGHS

The following chapters are full of the experiences and wisdom of individuals who have been mentors to me and to other successful Producers all over the nation. I have asked each of these contributing mentors of mine to share what they have learned through their individual Soul Purpose journeys, and what living their Soul Purpose has led them to. They were gracious enough to agree to share their personal stories and discoveries with the readers of this book.

Every contributor has inspired me, and has directly contributed to my personal success, and they can do the same for you. I have met with hundreds of high-level players across the spectrum of the financial services industry, and I can truly say that these individuals are the people who are the very best at what they do. In a sense, this book is an assembly of your own personal "board of directors". You have a truly marvelous opportunity to glean personal insights from their experiences and breakthroughs. This book reveals an the incredible philosophy of Soul Purpose from many angles, and walks of life, which can help you to become clearer about your own Soul Purpose, and the paths that you will take.

I want you to understand how valuable this opportunity to read their stories is, so that you can get the most out if. These amazing, successful people are sharing highly personal experiences, and great wisdom accrued through their lives and Soul Purpose journeys. This book is a highly concentrated dosage of specialized wisdom and inspiration that no one person could ever discover entirely on their own in one lifetime. Allow yourself to absorb this knowledge, and leverage the expertise of these remarkable Producers. If you do so, I can promise; you will experience some incredible breakthroughs of your own.

You can contact me at: garrett@freedomfasttrack.com.

# CHAPTER 2

# GARRETT WHITE

## The Investors paradigm, LLC.

*Garrett is the President of The Investors Paradigm Inc., a multi-million dollar corporation dedicated to teaching individuals to create wealth in all areas of their lives: financially, relationally, intellectually, physically and spiritually by understanding principles of prosperity.*

*Since his beginning 5 years ago Garrett has devoted over 5 years to studying the thoughts, actions, and habits of those who possess true wealth in all areas of their lives. Just as those studies, Garrett has created an impressive list of his own successes, including playing football at the collegiate level for Boise State University, competing in full distance Iron Man triathlons, building two multi-million dollar mortgage companies, top honors in the Mortgage Planning arenas in the state of Nevada and the state of Utah, Coach and Mentor to some of the Top Mortgage Planning and Financial Planning advisors around the country, Speaking in over 50 cities in 2006 to literally thousands of individuals, sharing the stage with top speakers the likes of Omar Periu, Raymond Aaron, Robert Sheeman, Wayne Gray, Garrett Gunderson and many more.*

*Garrett has studied and been exposed to a wide diversity of teachings and teachers – from traditional college and the schools of the corporate world, to the spiritual teachings of powerful religious leaders the world over. As a result, he has the unique ability to blend the spiritual power of principles of wealth and the practical strategies and actions steps into a usable and easy to access formula.*

*As a Top Mortgage Planner, Coach, Trainer, Speaker, Mentor and Radio Show Host, Garrett has taught thousands of individuals and organizations to create wealth in all areas of their business and lives by assisting them through a process of breaking down old paradigms and replacing them with updated paradigms based on eternal principles of prosperity.*

*When he is not attending Seminars or receiving coaching or mentoring from his financial and spiritual teachers, Garrett spends time creating as much value for as many people as he possibly can – starting with his beautiful wife Danielle, and his son Parker and Daughter Bailey who reside in Salt lake City, Utah.*

## TIMELESS PRINCIPLES

The fundamental, timeless principles on which the creation of wealth and all success in life are based, such as Soul Purpose, Stewardship, and Value Creation, all tend to enhance and reinforce one another. Living Soul Purpose is really just Stewardship of one's inborn talents and passions. Soul Purpose is expressed within a specific vocation through the Creation of Value for others. Value Creation itself is the result of Stewardship of one's knowledge and experience within a vocation.

There are critical distinctions between each of these timeless principles, however. Soul Purpose results in Creation of Value through Stewardship. But, Soul Purpose is neither Creation of Value, nor Stewardship alone. Soul Purpose is not a single vocation. Rather, it is the combination of a person's inborn abilities and passion, directed toward a purpose of great personal meaning. Soul Purpose can be expressed through a myriad of vocations, many of which might be totally unrelated to one another, but which all employ a person's unique abilities, and which all inspire similar passions. In this way, finding Soul Purpose is more about finding self, than it is about finding the right job.

I try to be a powerful example of Soul Purpose, Stewardship, and Value Creation in action. As Co-Founder and Partner of The Investors Paradigm, my work touches the lives of thousands of clients annually, by teaching them how to be powerful Stewards of the equity in their homes by 'Acting Like a Bank' through the application of the economic principles of Leverage, Arbitrage, Utilization, and Velocity.

The following pages will define these concepts in great detail, and describe the process through which The Investors Paradigm takes its clients. First, however, I will tell about my own Soul Purpose journey, which will hopefully give greater insight into Soul Purpose as a fundamental principle of success, and its expression through Stewardship and Value Creation.

## A SHATTERED DREAM

Since my first memories, my life has always been about the pursuit of excellence in football. As an eight year-old boy, I remember an adult asking me what I wanted to be when I grew up. My immediate reply was, "I'm going to be a BYU football player!" The man looked down at me and said, "There's no way!" That day I decided to not believe him, and a new belief was created. I committed myself to achieving anything I desired, no matter what other people said.

My parents reinforced this commitment and taught me that, when I wanted something, it was my responsibility to get it. They lived this creed themselves, and were hard workers and fine examples. They never discouraged me from my dreams of college and professional football, and instilled in me the discipline and confidence required to accomplish these goals and anything else I put my mind to. After great success in high school football, and careful consideration of my best course of action, I went on to play for Boise University, then professionally in Canada and The National Indoor Football League. With these successes established, I redoubled my efforts, intent on reaching the Mecca of professional football, the NFL.

What came next destroyed those dreams, and shook me to the very core of my personal identity. I was diagnosed with cancer.

In a life designed and dedicated for physical excellence, I felt for the first time unclear, uncertain and like I was losing control. I had fixed a goal in my mind since childhood, and built the drive and direction required to achieve it. Then, all of a sudden, that goal was rendered impossible, and even meaningless. My life was at stake. Suddenly football seemed inconsequential.

## FINDING SOUL PURPOSE

After nine major surgeries, my cancer was successfully eliminated. The psychological damage took a bit longer to overcome, however. I was faced with a full-scale redefinition of my life's purpose. I could not return to playing pro-fessional football, but football was all I had known my entire life. What was I going to do now?

I spent long hours analyzing my situation. I was young, had a college degree in Physical Education, was an expert at football and only football, and enjoyed helping people. I decided my first "real job" would be coaching high school football and teaching PE. With my history of personal accomplishment and expertise, I got a job easily.

I soon realized that I loved coaching. I did not, however, love teaching PE to high school students who obviously did not want to be in my class. This was my first lesson in Soul Purpose. There's no use trying to force yourself to do something you distinctly hate; you only poison the experience for yourself and others around you. Better to focus on and improve your strengths and passions than spend your time becoming mediocre at uninteresting weaknesses.

One day, I had a conversation with several other football coaches, most of whom had been working in secondary education for 15 to 20 years. This discussion came after a teacher meeting during which the Principal had announced another up-coming pay cut. These coaches were already making so little money that they had to look for income opportunities outside of school. One taught driver's education on the side; another taught computer classes just to provide for his family. These coaches were frustrated and struggling with the idea of doing what they loved but not getting the money or respect they believed they deserved.

As they sat there upset and arguing, I posed a somewhat rhetorical set of questions: "Man, are we going to ever get free doing this? Can we get rich? Can we be wealthy doing this?" One of the coaches looked at me and said: "You're young, so get out while you can." I was blown away. These were the very men that were supposed to inspire me to commit fully to my work. Instead they were telling me to abandon it, and wishing they themselves had done so years earlier.

Trusting these men's advice, and my own gut instincts, I began looking into other job opportunities. I knew I wanted to make a good living, and had become more convinced than ever that my true passion in life came from helping other people achieve something they wouldn't have been able to do without my advice and coaching. All I had ever known was football, but I had come to realize that my expertise in football was just a tool for helping others. Football was just a vehicle to achieve a much larger purpose, helping people. I realized that, if coaching football couldn't provide the life I wanted for my future family, and for myself, I would have to find another vehicle, another tool that would. This vocation had to offer me the opportunity for wealth, but still allow me to help others. In turn, I would have to commit myself to becoming an expert in it, just as I had dedicated my life up until then to football.

## A NEW PATH

Around this same time, a friend introduced I to the idea of becoming a mortgage broker. I didn't know exactly what a mortgage broker was, but agreed to interview for a position with my friend's company nonetheless. In preparation for the meeting, I was told to read a book called Rich Dad, Poor Dad by Robert Kiyosaki. I read the book three times in seven days. This was the fifth book I had read in my entire life.

Kiyosaki opened my mind to a whole new world of possibilities that I had never been taught. These were principles and concepts of wealth that had always existed, but had never been introduced to in my entire life. Reading Rich Dad, Poor Dad allowed me to see these possibilities for the first time. My first reading sparked an ember of hope for my own future. By the time I finished my third reading, that ember had become a bonfire. I went to my interview with a newfound enthusiasm for the mortgage industry that had rivaled my lifelong love of football. I was offered the job, and quickly became one of the company's most prolific agents.

Within a year, I was making more money on a monthly basis than I had made in the previous year. When you make money you begin to meet people who are similarly ambitious and successful. I believe this is no coincidence. When the student is ready, the teacher will appear. Mentors began to come into my life and taught me about real estate. I learned about banking and arbitrage. I began to realize that the way I had structured my own home financing, and the way I was encouraging my clients to structure theirs, was destructive to our financial well being.

## LIFE LESSONS—THE LAW OF THE LID

The first time I purchased a home, several well-meaning friends and family members coached me on my new mortgage. "You've got a nice home now honey, and we are so excited for you!" my grandmother told me. "Now you have to get that thing paid off just as soon as you possibly can."

I believed this advice, because I loved the people giving it to me, and I knew they had my best interest at heart. Also, they had a history of giving me good advice as I was growing up. Because it was the only advice I was hearing at the time, I naturally assumed that it must be correct.

Thinking I was helping them achieve security by owning their homes quicker, I directed my clients into mortgage products with 15-year repayment periods, and encouraged them to make biweekly payments. When an insightful client would question my reasoning, I would defend my advice by saying, only half-jokingly, "Because my grandma said so." If the client pressed further, asking why my grandma says so, I would stretch the joke further, "Well, because her mom said so."

The truth was that I didn't really know why paying off a mortgage quickly was the best approach to creating wealth or home ownership. I had been told that mortgages were a threat to the American Dream of home ownership, and that financial security came only from paying them off as quickly as possible. Intuitively, this logic didn't really make complete sense to me, but it was the only rationale I had been offered.

Despite my lack of certainty, I nonetheless repeated this logic to my clients, which was actually a course of action that I now know to be destructive. I relate my own behavior, and that of anyone who has a similarly structured mortgage without knowing why, to a story I first heard from Omar Periu, called "The Law of the Lid."

At a college research laboratory some years ago, a group of scientists were studying the learning processes of insects and other so-called "unsophisticated" animals. They performed a wide variety of experiments, expecting to demonstrate that any adaptive behaviors "learned" by these animals would be only temporary, and that instinctive behaviors would quickly resume once the force that motivated the behavioral change was removed. The scientists were surprised to learn the exact opposite was true.

One such experiment involved fleas in a jar. When the fleas were first put into the jar, they immediately began to jump out. When a scientist put a lid on the jar, the fleas initially jumped into the lid, attempting to escape. Quickly, however, the fleas "learned" to jump lower than the lid and avoid the painful headaches that followed such bumping. The interesting part of this study is that when the lid was removed some time later, the fleas continued to jump below that level as if the lid were still there. This behavior was not only pointless, but willfully self-defeating, and prevented the fleas from fulfilling their desire to escape. Yet, even after many hours without a lid to constrain their escape, these fleas continued to jump just high enough to not bump into the lid that was no longer there.

We highly sophisticated humans do the same thing. We're taught the level of the "lid" in all areas of our lives, and we confine our behaviors to those activities that won't have us bumping into the nonexistent glass ceilings limiting our success.

This "law of the lid" had me following and repeating pointless and destructive advice to my mortgage clients that first year in business. The reality I was convincing my clients of, the nonexistent lid I was teaching them to fear, was the assumption that home "ownership" is worthwhile, that it is the only way to achieve financial security, and that the only way to achieve home ownership itself is to pay off the mortgage on the home as quickly as possible.

These assumptions are all incorrect. That they are false, however, does not mean they aren't powerful. These faulty assumptions keep millions of homeowners trapped in a paradigm that prevents productive stewardship of one of their most important and lucrative resources, the equity in their homes and the ability to Act like a Bank!

## A REALIZATION BECOMES THE INVESTORS PARADIGM

The source of any genuine change in life is always the realization of one's previous belief in a lie. To be meaningful, this realization must demand an immediate change in behavior. I had realized, through my mentorship with others that already understood the timeless principles of wealth creation and success, that I was teaching untruth to my mortgage clients. This realization demanded an immediate change in my behavior. That change resulted in The Investors Paradigm. I left my work with the mortgage company where I had worked for the previous year, and launched The Investors Paradigm with several partners. Ever since, our collective mission has been to turn the mortgage industry upside-down.

The Investors Paradigm is unique in the mortgage industry. Where most mortgage companies expect to work with a client only once, The Investors Paradigm closes loans for clients sometimes dozens of times. Where most mortgage companies compete with one another on price and offer no distinguishing client experience, The Investors Paradigm focuses exclusively on client experience and its mortgage planners never worry that they will lose clients to other companies. Where most mortgage companies tell clients which product is best, The Investors Paradigm educates its clients on the timeless principles of wealth creation, and then lets those clients choose their own mortgage product.

The cornerstone of The Investors Paradigm is a process called The Full Investors Experience, during which clients are taught the fundamental principles of wealth creation. Individuals interested in a complete explanation of The Full Investors Experience can find more information by clicking on the "F.I.E." link at www.TheInvestorsParadigm.com. The following pages will detail some of the most important principles taught to clients of The Full Investors Experience, and how those principles can help a client choose the right mortgage to maximize the production and utilization of home equity.

## PERSPECTIVE DETERMINES ACTION

Our perspective of the world is based upon our current paradigms. Paradigms are the filters through which we interpret the world, and are created through knowledge, past experience, and the influence of others. Parents, teachers, friends, and anyone else who we love and listen to, teach us our paradigms. One of the most prominent financial paradigms is that money is evil, that money is the root of all evil, that money is scarce (doesn't grow on trees), and that the reason certain people are not wealthy is because they are virtuous.

These beliefs shape people's behavior, because it is difficult to embrace the creation of wealth if one thinks money is evil. Most people want money, but feel guilty about acquiring it, even honestly. They want what money can produce, but are taught that it is cankerous and destructive. These opinions and assumptions work together to create a belief system. People with this belief system return to it as a frame of reference every time they make a decision about money. The decisions then determine their perspective on the world and their behaviors.

Beliefs create behaviors, which create results. If I am dissatisfied with my current results, I cannot simply change my behaviors and expect different results. I must first address the root cause of my behaviors themselves, my beliefs.

## THE AHA MOMENT

The first, and most dramatic action The Investors Paradigm has its clients take is to question their own beliefs about mortgages. What do they believe? Why do they believe that? How did they learn these beliefs?

Most clients share the typical belief system that would have them pay off their mortgage as quickly as possible, and then save the money that previously went to their payment. As they begin to unravel the deceptive nature of these beliefs, the truth comes forward, and an amazing thing happens. These clients begin to form a new perspective. The Investors Paradigm calls this an "aha moment," when the lie becomes obvious and the truth emerges, a "Paradigm Shift."

From my experience teaching hundreds and thousands of individuals, I have observed that every single person falls into one of two general categories in their belief system about money. People are either Consumers or Producers.

## THE CONSUMER CONDITION

Consumers believe that money is scarce, and access to money is limited. Because money is scarce, consumers believe that material possessions and money have inherent value. By their logic, the more money, or the more material possessions these consumers can hoard, the more "wealthy" they are. Consumers fail to see that nothing in life has value until we as human beings assign value to it.

In addition, consumers attempt to take value from others. They consume as much as possible, without giving back. They feel entitled to things without working for them. When they don't receive these things, or are forced to work for them, consumers see themselves as victims. They are also paranoid that everyone is out to get them. The mortgage company is out to get them. Their spouse is out to get them, their neighbor is out to get them, everyone is out to take advantage of them and when anything negative happens to them, they claim that another person is at fault.

Because perspective determines actions, the consumer treats money and material possessions with greater respect than human life. Consumers express these misguided priorities in two characteristic ways, which The Investors Paradigm calls The Spender and The Saver. Each of these consumer types is motivated by an "Emotional Governing Directive," which is a fancy term that simply means that the consumer uses money to achieve a certain pleasurable emotion, or avoid a certain painful emotion. Spenders and Savers just give different emotions higher priority. To analyze each type of consumer, let's give him $1000 and see what he does with it.

## THE SPENDER

A Spender's Emotional Governing Directive is immediate gratification. Immediate gratification means that a Spender doesn't want something yesterday, or two days from now. The Spender wants it today, and is unwilling to wait until financial circumstances fit with desires. A Spender with a sudden influx of $1000 will "Blow It."

Not only will a Spender spend the $1000 in hand, but that Spender will likely blow a few hundred dollars more, racking up credit card debt. This debt doesn't mean much to the Spender, because it's a promise of future repayment. "Future" is a vague and meaningless term to a Spender. The Spender only knows present, and pleasure in the present. His life is driven by immediate gratification. When money comes in or a resource is available, the Spender consumes it as quickly as possible.

## THE SAVER

The Emotional Governing Directive for a Saver, on the other hand, is safety and security. Given $1,000, a Saver might look at the spender and think, "You're insane. How could you blow money like that?" Hence, the Saver does the opposite of the Spender. The Saver says, "No way am I going to blow this $1000. I am going to pay something off because if I owe any money to anyone, for any reason, it threatens my security and that is not okay with me."

## LEARNING TO BE A SAVER/SPENDER

Most Consumers don't recognize their own Emotional Governing Directive. Likewise, most Consumers don't realize that both of these mindsets are taught. They are learned by experience. If you were raised in a household that believed that the sky was falling, fear of loss dominated, and/or scarcity dominated your household, then it is likely that you are a Saver or a Spender.

## THE PRODUCER PERSPECTIVE

The alternative to Consumerist, Spender/Saver behavior is the Producer Perspective. Producers believe that the resources of life are abundant, not scarce. They believe there is plenty of money, opportunity, time, energy, love, and everything else of value available for everyone. Producers believe that life itself is meant to be lived abundantly, graciously, generously, and haply. They place value in principle and people, and realize that money and material possessions are only tools to achieve human happiness. In the mind of the Producer, people, not things, have intrinsic value. Things are merely the resources or tools that are useful to produce value for people.

Producers also believe that Dollars Follow Value. When Producers want to create more wealth, they do so by focusing their efforts on creating value that can be exchanged with other people. They create this value by utilizing and maximizing whatever resources are available to them. Common resources that Producers use to create value include: money, real estate, home equity, businesses, machinery, knowledge, experience, relationships, employees, trustworthiness, and many others. In reality, the resources available to a Producer are only limited by that Producer's imagination. The most powerful Producers are those who can identify the potential to create the most value from even the most unlikely resources. This is a skill that all Producers work to cultivate.

Unlike Consumers, Producers feel empowered to control the circumstances of their lives, and never complain that they are the victims of another, or are entitled to wealth without work. The Producer acts as a Steward of everything he or she owns or controls, including the equity in his or her home.

When Producers identify resources, they analyze how these resources can be invested most wisely. This type of thinking is called The Investors Paradigm, and is motivated by a very empowering Emotional Governing Directive: the desire to be free. An Investor given $1000 will dedicate it to achieving freedom. They are unwilling to "Blow It" like a Spender, and uninspired by the false sense of security a Saver gets at the expense of Return on Investment (ROI). The Producer is much like the two Stewards in the parable of the talents that Christ gave in The Bible, who exercise their talents and multiply their resources. The Investor will invest the $1000 in assets that produce value for others, and income for one's self. When enough assets have been purchased or created, the monthly expenses of the Producer are covered by the income from those assets. This is called Financial Freedom. To the Productive Investors, Financial Freedom is the permission slip to dedicate one's self to a lifelong process of personal growth, focused on increasing one's ability to create more value for others.

## THE SPENDER'S MORTGAGE

Like all behaviors, the unique ways a Spender, Saver, and Investor manage a sudden influx of $1000, are based on their belief systems about money. These belief systems are not limited to money alone, however. They also govern their behaviors in relation to all types of resources, including home equity.

The Spender views their home as a black hole where money that could be used for immediate gratification goes to die. Making a monthly mortgage payment eats at a Spender. That's just less money for shopping for the latest trendy clothes or a new car.

Likewise, a Spender will quickly cash out and spend any equity in my home for immediate gratification. In the past four or five years, appreciation in the national housing market has been unprecedented. High appreciation means large amounts of equity. Spenders nationwide have heard the ka-ching of their home equity payday, and gone to refinance their homes as quickly as possible.

The banking institutions around the country do everything in their power to market to this Spender group because it makes up roughly 60-70% of the American public. Banks convince Spenders to use home equity to consolidate credit card bills, go on a vacation, buy a new car, or remodel their homes. Banks structure the terms of their mortgages to let Spenders pull this off. 125% Loan-to-Value loans, second mortgages, third mortgages, lines of credit, 30-year fixed mortgages, and others all encourage the Spender to refinance over and over again to meet that emotional need of immediate gratification. Spenders take advantage of these programs, and quickly blow their cashed-out home equity on material possessions that give them pleasure only until the next fancy trinket catches their eye. A month after their loan closes, Spenders have nothing to show for the home equity they have squandered.

## THE SAVER'S MORTGAGE

A Saver wants nothing more than to "own" my home outright. To the Saver, "ownership" means having no mortgage on the property. As such, a Saver sacrifices all other desires and opportunities to pay off my home as quickly as possible.

The Saver Paradigm is a holdover from The Great Depression, when banks could call loans due whenever they wanted, leaving families homeless and devastated. Modern mortgages can't be called due like this, but the obsessive fear of homelessness still directs the Saver's behavior. The saver pays off his or her home to feel safe and secure from a threat that no longer exists. Even if a Saver knows the loan can't be called due without contractual cause, the Saver creates other fears to avoid. A Saver fears what might happen if he or she loses a job, or fears an accident or emergency that might make one unable to make one's mortgage payment. Instead of addressing these unlikely scenarios with insurance and consistent value creation, the Saver compulsively struggles to pay off my mortgage and own all property outright.

The Saver is not concerned so much about a large outstanding balance of the mortgage. In fact, the smaller the amount he owes on my mortgage, the more obsessed the Saver becomes about paying it off. This is because his real fear is the monthly payment, and the possibility of losing one's home if the payment can't be made. The only course of action for the Saver is to eliminate this payment entirely. He will structure his mortgage to do this as quickly as possible, using a 30, 20, or even 15-year fixed mortgage, perhaps making bi-weekly payments, and pre-paying the balance down with any extra money he comes into.

## THE INVESTOR'S MORTGAGE

The Investor is not governed by the desire for immediate gratification or security. Instead, he or she is motivated by the achievement of freedom. Home equity is viewed as a resource, just like any other tool of production. She structures her mortgage to take advantage of this resource within a comprehensive financial plan designed to achieve financial freedom as quickly as possible.

Critically, the Investor does not focus on "owning" one's home, but rather "controlling" it as a resource of production. He or she does not have to make decisions based on emotion. Emotion and economics are two different things. The Spender and the Saver are blinded and deceived by emotion. The Investor maintains clarity and perspective to make informed, thoughtful decisions. He can look objectively at the circumstances of his life and say "Wow, this might work better a different way, I might be a better steward over my resource if I did something else."

To the Spender, home equity represents a $100,000 payday. The Saver views it as a step closer to total security. The Investor sees equity as potential to create value, for self, family, and for others.

## ANALYZING INVESTMENTS AS TOOLS OF PRODUCTION

The Investor analyzes the potential of the home equity as an investment. As a prudent investor, he or she asks four questions, which are applicable to any real estate transaction, or any investment decision at all.

**The four questions that Producers ask about any investment are:**

*1. How much liquidity does the investment offer?*

*2. Is the investment safe, and what are the risks involved?*

*3. What is the rate of return?*

*4. What are the secondary consequences, i.e. tax implications, opportunity cost, etc.?*

Investors analyze competing investment opportunities to decide where they should utilize their resources. Simply put, the best investments win. To decide whether to keep their home equity, or cash it out through refinance, Investors compare the two options as investments. First, they ask the four questions above about their home equity. It turns out that equity left in a home makes for a lousy investment.

Number one, home equity is not liquid. Liquidity is defined as the ability to access money when needed. Most Americans believe that their home equity is liquid and accessible anytime they need it. These people are sadly misinformed.

The events surrounding Hurricane Katrina illustrate how illiquid home equity is. A New Orleans couple was interviewed on the news immediately following the devastating floods there. They spoke of how they had received a financial windfall several weeks before the storm, and decided to invest this money in their own security by paying off their mortgage. These Savers believed that, if they really needed the money sometime in the future, they could simply take out another mortgage. They thought they were buying freedom, by ending their monthly mortgage payments.

Three weeks later, Hurricane Katrina hit. The levees broke and their home was destroyed. The insurance company claimed their loss was the result of flood damage, which was not covered. Not only was their house gone, but their recent financial windfall was gone too. Had they asked the bank to return their pre-paid mortgage to them, they would have got a polite denial, and provoked some sincere sympathy in the poor teller who had to deliver the news.

Home equity is not liquid. Acting like it is forces a person to react to circumstance instead of acting on opportunity. A wise Investor realizes that, at least by the criteria of this first question, keeping equity in a home makes for a bad investment decision.

The second question an Investor asks is whether Home Equity is a safe investment. To return to the previous example, the New Orleans couple prepaid several hundred thousand dollars to rid themselves of their mortgage, believing this made them safe and secure in their home. Obviously, this couple was wrong.

Even for those not at risk of natural disaster, the financial implications of keeping home equity trapped in the home place them at greater risk than other investments. When a person has fully paid off the mortgage on my home, this fully owned asset becomes a huge target in the event of a lawsuit. If I has not yet paid off my mortgage fully, every dollar of equity I grows only makes the bank safer, and me less safe. If I were to encounter unexpected financial difficulty, the Saver with substantial home equity would be the first person the bank would foreclose on. The Saver's home, worth much more than the amount owed on it, would be easy to sell on the open market. The bank could quickly recapture its loaned funds. Alternatively, a bank holding a note at 95% or 100% of a property's value will do everything in its power not to fore-close, because the bank realizes it will never get back what it owes on the property when it is sold at auction.

For these reasons, home equity actually puts the Saver at greater risk than leveraging that equity for other investing purposes.

There must be other reasons that make home equity a great investment, though, to compensate for it being illiquid and unsafe. Right?

Question number three asks "What is the rate of return on the investment?" Sadly for Savers, the rate of return on home equity is always 0%. To verify this, ask yourself when you will be paid by, or for, your home equity. The answer, of course, is never. Home equity doesn't send its owner checks every month. Likewise, a person's home equity grows based on the appreciation of the home's value, not based on the amount of equity already in the home. That equity, sitting unused and gathering metaphorical dust, actually loses value as inflation eats away at its purchasing power.

The only way to activate passive equity is to do one of two things: mortgage the home and pull the money out in a loan, or sell the property. Neither of these options fit well with either of the Consumer Saver perspectives on money.

However, the Productive Investor thinks more creatively. He asks, "How can I earn a rate of return on my home equity? How can I activate it? I've got to get it liquid, I've got to get it safe, and I have to get it working for me in an investment opportunity that is producing a high rate of return." By asking the right questions and acting accordingly, the Investor achieves productivity where the Saver and Spender create only stagnation.

The last question an Investor asks is about the secondary consequences of an investment. The most obvious of these consequences are the tax implications. What are the tax benefits of home equity? Simply put, home equity creates no tax deduction. The Saver thinks this is an acceptable loss, for the feeling of (false) security home equity gives me. The Producer knows that cashing out my home equity through a mortgage not only gives me access to low-interest money that I can then invest for higher interest, but it also lets me deduct the interest I pays on that mortgage from my taxes.

The four questions a Productive Investor asks about any investment spell bad news for home equity. It is not liquid, not safe, has no rate of return and no tax benefits. Upon figuring this out, the wise Investor rushes to the bank to cash out equity through a properly structured mortgage. He or she then takes this cashed-out equity and transfers it to an investment that gives exciting answers to the previous four questions.

When an Investor does this, she is actually acting just like a bank. She is borrowing money at low interest, and investing it to earn high interest. The investor is achieving something called Arbitrage.

## LEVERAGE & ARBITRAGE –
## WINNING BIG WITH OTHER PEOPLE'S MONEY

Because Investors understand the principle of Leverage and Arbitrage, they are able to play partners with the banks as opposed to victims. Imagine that an Investor refinances her home and cashes out $100,000 in equity. She has automatically done something that no Saver would ever do. She also plans to invest the money for production, not consume it like a Spender. Instead, the Producer purchases an asset that produces enough income on a monthly basis to cover her mortgage payment. She performed her due diligence on this asset while she was refinancing, and structured her loan so that the payment was below the monthly income from the asset. In fact, her payment is lower than it previously was, even though she owes $100,000 more. She did all this through the power of Leverage & Arbitrage.

When an Investor works to establish Arbitrage, she looks at equity itself as a resource and is unafraid of borrowing from banks. Consider whether you would borrow money from a bank at 36% interest. The Spender would, and promptly Blow It. The Saver wouldn't even consider such a reckless financial maneuver. But the Producer would ask, "What interest could I earn on that money?" If that interest were more than 36%, taking the loan would ultimately be profitable.

As a real-world example of this, Larry H. Miller (the owner of the Utah Jazz and a large number of successful businesses around the country) borrowed money to build the Delta Center when conventional rates were near 20%. Was he crazy? Not at all, since the investment was based using economic principles. The Utah Jazz is now worth almost $500 million. Producers know Arbitrage is all about comparing the interest they pay to get the interest they earn.

Investors realize that, whether they want to or not, they take part in this Arbitrage game daily. Consider this example: For your hard work, your employer gives you a $5,000 bonus. If you are a Spender, you go straight to the Check Cashing Center, fork over $300 to cash your check, and Blow It in Vegas. If you're a Saver, you buy $5000 worth of home equity that sits idle, earning 0% interest, but making you feel safe until the levees break.

But, if you're an Investor, you go to the bank, deposit your money in your checking account, and begin analyzing various investment opportunities. You want to be wise with your money, so it will take a few days or weeks to decide where to invest it.

In the meantime, the bank takes your money and does its own investing. They gladly accept your deposit, and are even willing to pay you 0.75% for your money. They then turn around and loan that money to someone else, typically a Spender on my way to the mall, for between 5% and 25%. The bank has achieved Arbitrage with your $5,000.

Most people don't realize that when they deposit money into a checking account, they are actually making a loan to the bank. The bank makes it so easy to do, it doesn't seem like a loan. Most loans require a lot of paperwork, notarized signatures, and practically a laser eye scan to prove you will repay! That's the beauty of the bank's Arbitrage: they make it easy for you to give them your money, and ensure through substantial due diligence that they will earn higher interest when they loan that money out to someone else. Consider that, if a bank pays 1% interest on a checking account, and then turns around and earns 7% interest on a home mortgage with that money, that bank is not earning a 6% rate of return. It is actually earning 6 times what it spends (not considering the bank's business expenses). That is a 600% rate of return on its money. That is Leverage and Arbitrage in action.

An old adage says "There are only two types of people in this world, those who pay interest and those who earn interest." The Investor turns this adage on its head, and adds a third category of people: those who pay interest in order to make interest. Arbitrage is merely the ability to borrow other people's money at a specific rate and to put that money to work in a productive manner earning a higher interest rate. The difference between these interest rates is the Producer's to keep. An Investor uses the equity in my home to be the bank. The home merely becomes collateral for him to utilize the resource of other people's money. This is why banking institutions continue to profit. And investors understand it, and benefit too. Shouldn't you as well?

## MONEY IN MOTION...THE MULTIPLIER EFFECT

The Investor is light years ahead of the Saver and the Spender in his financial wisdom. He uses the equity in his home as collateral to secure low-interest loans from banks. He then uses these loans to invest in assets that earn monthly income, which pays any increase in his monthly payment. In all likelihood, however, the Investor's mortgage payment is no more than the Spender's or Saver's, even though he has borrowed substantially more money. He takes advantage of specific loan structures that reduce his monthly liability, so he can keep as much of his own money as possible, which he also wisely invests.

The Investor is still unsatisfied, however. He is forever on the watch for greater opportunity to maximize the productivity of his resources. One day the Investor gets an amazing idea: I will simply use the same dollar twice, three times, or as many times as possible. I will just multiply my money.

This "Multiplier Effect" is also practiced with great skill by banks. The Federal Reserve requires that banks maintain a reserve of only 10% of the total amount of money they have issued as loans to borrowers, at any given time. That means that a bank can loan out every dollar in its vault nine times. The bank uses the same resources for multiple purposes simultaneously. And, so do Investor's.

For example, an Investor might cash out and invest his home equity into income-producing assets. She then uses the income from those assets to pay the monthly premium on a Whole Life insurance policy. That insurance policy accrues Cash Value, which the Investor owns and can borrow against at low interest rates. In this way, the Cash Value of the insurance policy is similar to the Equity in the Investor's home. She cashes it out and invests it into more income-producing assets. The Investor repeats this cycle indefinitely, earning interest from interest from interest.

This is only one example of how a Producer might take advantage of The Multiplier Effect. The specifics of this example might work in certain situations, and be ineffective in others. The important thing is that the Investor knows how to analyze investment opportunities to know when she can earn interest at a higher rate than she pays to borrow money for the investment.

## A CALL TO ACTION

All achievement in life comes from a simple formula: Be > Do > Have. One must first commit mentally, psychologically, and spiritually to "being" a Productive Investor. This commitment to "being" naturally results in behaviors aligned with "The Investors Paradigm." This is the "doing" portion. These behaviors naturally bring about the results a Productive Investor receives. These are the "haves": success, wealth, health, and happiness.

As a young child, I committed to being a person who could not be deterred from my dreams. This led me to a career in professional football. When this career was cut short by cancer, I committed again, to being someone whose life is devoted to creating value for others. I committed a third time to being an expert in mortgages just as I was an expert in football. I combined all of these commitments to achieve my Soul Purpose in my chosen vocation: helping others to realize financial freedom by using their Home Equity as a resource of production.

The message I bring to the world, and the principles I teach my clients, extend far beyond the realm of home equity and mortgages, however. My company, The Investors Paradigm, teaches people how to contribute to others in the local and global marketplace, by creating maximum value through Stewardship of their resources. The Investors Paradigm directly helps clients to make use of their home equity as a resource. But, the lessons of Value Creation are applicable to all resources and in all situations.

I invite you, as someone who is obviously committed to personal growth and value creation yourself, to investigate The Investors Paradigm further. An audio recording of The One Night Retirement event can be downloaded free of charge from www.TheInvestorsParadigm.com. Additionally, The Investors Paradigm offers free one-hour one-on-one consultations with its expert mortgage planners.

You can contact me at: gwhite@theaccreditednetwork.com, or 1-800-400-5206.

# CHAPTER 3

# STEVE D'ANNUNZIO
## The Prosperity Paradigm, LLC.

*Steve D'Annunzio is a behavior modification teacher who mentors life success coaches all over the country. His radically effective teachings pull people "out of their minds and into their hearts." Steve uses principles of Higher Awareness to inspire others to be far greater versions of themselves than they ever knew to be possible. By combining scientific and spiritual truth, he co-creates inner transformations for people to experience more outer prosperity in their life. He is an author and composer of many books, paradigms, and artistic projects that have the common theme of alleviating human suffering and enhancing joy. He has recently finished his latest book, The Prosperity Paradigm. Steve lives with his family in Rochester, New York.*

## SOUL PURPOSE DISTINCTIONS

Soul purpose is your unique series of talents, strengths, passions, interests, hobbies, attitudes, and values that form the essence of the most magnificent version of you. When these qualities are intentionally acknowledged and cultivated, they coalesce into a specific mission in service to the world. These qualities already exist within you in a basic raw form. For most people they need to be clearly discovered, then nourished, studied and refined. Soul purpose is like gold – hidden deep within, but when painstakingly sought for and carefully mined – makes for fabulous wealth.

The common denominator of all successful and famous people throughout history is that they all lived their soul purpose. They all 'followed their bliss' – daring, many times against impossible odds, to be that which they believed they were destined to become. This bliss led them to do what they had an innate passion and talent for. Their cause became a life mission – a raison d'etre. They rarely set out to achieve fame and fortune. On the contrary, fame and fortune occurred as 'effects,' stemming from each person following their inborn 'cause.' This cause became their guiding beacon whenever fear, doubt, and worry assailed them. It guided them to have faith, and the will to persist in times of challenge.

Most people come to recognize the relevance and validity of soul purpose only after experiencing great discontent. This discontent stems from not living their life with purpose. They know they're here to do something important but all they can say is that they're definitely not doing it. Thus, discontent acts as the fuel that propels people towards the discovery of this concept. We come to soul purpose by discovering who we are not, and do not, want to be and do. Thus it is important to also address what soul purpose is not;

*a job*

*a career*

*about money*

*about fame*

*about material things*

*without struggle*

*easy*

*glamorous*

*indicative of any 'special ness'*

*worthy of any adulation but simple respect*

The phrase soul purpose is derived from realizing that you are a soul in a body who has a mind. While residing in a material body and using the mind as a computer for storing, retrieving and analyzing data, the soul is your true essence. But because of very deeply ingrained cultural conditioning, we have forgotten the essence of that which we really are. This conditioning drastically hinders people's belief in themselves and their possibilities in the world. The following story illustrates this point.

In India, elephants are still used for many heaving-lifting tasks. When the elephants are in training they are secured by a thick chain to a one-foot wide steel shaft cemented deep into the ground. As the trainer begins teaching them they initially pull and pull trying to free themselves, but after a couple weeks the elephant realizes it's useless and stops pulling. From that point forward the trainer can lead them around by a string! This massively strong creature has been conditioned for the rest of its life to never change, because of its early conditioning. Human beings are very similar. This conditioning causes us to look at the world in a very fixed and limited way, without our even knowing it. So we forget our essence and settle for a life of mediocrity. I believe this is the root of why so many good people experience depression—their soul is so stifled that it is crying our for the expression of its real purpose.

## SOUL PURPOSE RESIDES IN THE SPIRITUAL REALM

One of the most important, and misunderstood, concepts surrounding Soul purpose is that it can only fully be lived when one accesses the spiritual realm. This is dicey business, discussing spirituality in a world in which that word has become such a controversial buzzword. So you understand the context, I use the word spirituality with the following meaning.

Spirituality is a way of being that people choose, or do not choose, every moment of their existence. It is choosing to be, and to behave, as either the God-Self or the ego-self. Studying the attributes to these two very different selves will be helpful for clarity sake.

| God-Self | ego-self |
|---|---|
| love | fear |
| confidence | worry |
| faith | doubt |
| learning | blaming |
| serving | prideful |
| humble | narcissistic |
| asking | demanding |
| empowering | controlling |
| Thy way | my way |

Thus, being spiritual is choosing love (power) over fear (force) when you are challenged. It is choosing to have faith instead of allowing ourselves to be filled with doubt when difficulties arise. When things don't go as planned the spiritual being focuses on learning instead of blaming, and so on with both categories of opposite qualities being virtually endless.

One can see that being spiritual may or may not have anything to do with religion, though the two words are often used interchangeably. According to the definition given here, many so-called religious people are anything but spiritual. Truly religious people are spiritual, but not all spiritual people practice a specific, or any, religion. The spiritual seeker focuses on the universal principles and values that form the basis of all religions, without the need of dogma or ecclesiastic approval. By committing to live these principles, the spiritually-oriented person gains entrance into a new field of life possibility. This field of possibility is the spiritual realm, which I will address more fully in a bit. While I am a huge proponent of the upside of religious life, it's necessary to illustrate the huge difference between religion and spirituality. Any sensible human being has great respect for the upside of religion, while also recognizing its downside. From the good works of a variety of differing religious groups people all over world have received food, clothing, medicine, and shelter in dire circumstances, and this is obviously very good. The downside of religion is a dangerous distortion wrought by fundamental fanatics who use it as a political control weapon hiding behind the cloak of scripture.

It is recognized that all religions are based upon the inspired revelations of an individual. Each was originally a great spiritual leader who inspired people through the radiance and presence of their own direct experience with Divinity (Spiritual Realm). This was the purpose of their being on Earth - it was their Soul purpose. Each one spoke from direct experience with God, not scriptural authority. However, with the death of each revelator, the original principles got distorted or were used out of context. Though the intentions of all religions were initially pure, the means by which the followers continued them became convoluted (mental realm).

The main error is honoring scripture more than God itself. Scripture is certainly a useful road map, but any traveler knows that the map is never the terrain. To deepen the confusion, each clan points to their own differing scripture claiming that it justifies their behavior. From this central error springs an 'us versus them' mentality that justifies negativity in the name of God. Negativity sucks people backwards into the mental realm of the ego-self. The ego-self seeks only to control, to be right, and to have its desires fulfilled. It doesn't care about love, which is the guiding ethic behind any true religion; it merely hides behind the banner of justified hostility in the name of God. When the purity emanating from the God-self becomes warped through the satanic lens of the ego, it twists the thinking processes towards paranoid schizophrenia. So what began as a Soul purpose mission beautifully transmitted from the spiritual domain, became a game of mind control issuing from the mental realm.

The folly of that might be best explained using this metaphor. Imagine driving on a family trip to the Grand Canyon. You buy a map outlining the most direct route there, complete with great pictures of the destination itself. You set out, following your map implicitly as it takes you around traffic snarls and proves its utility to the degree that you begin to become enamored, even attached, to it. Three days later you finally arrive at your original destination. But instead of getting out and hiking, exploring and experiencing the whole purpose of your journey, you just sit in your car pouring adoration onto the map. Your adoration is interrupted as a car pulls in next to yours. Your license plates say New York and the car next to yours has plates from California. You notice the driver adoring his map too. You think you have something in common with him so you get out to chat about the greatness of the map. You are dismayed however, to discover he has an entirely different map even though it accurately led him to the exact same place where you currently are. Because he drove from a different starting point his map must be different, which of course makes perfect sense to anyone thinking clearly. But you put all your faith into your map to the degree that you are completely attached, so you are no longer thinking clearly. Despite the fact that you both arrived at your intended destination, you decide to argue about whose map is right. And the more you try to convince each other you're right and he's wrong the angrier each one gets. Now a fight breaks out. So here you are in this magnificent sacred setting totally ignorant of the initial intention of the journey, trying to kill each other.

Look at the Protestants and Catholics in Ireland. Look at the Arabs and Jews in the Holy Land. Observe the Hindus and Muslims warring on the border of India and Pakistan, or the religious civil war between Shi'ite and Sunni in Iraq even though they're both Islamic. This is what many religions have become.

Notice that religious beliefs focus on accentuating differences, proving others wrong, moral superiority, and converting others. Each has a unique story that offers converts an edge on Truth, often claiming all others as erroneous. This can result in close-minded and fearful behavior of other philosophies outside of their own, condemning them as wrong with little or no knowledge of that which they condemn. Thus, religions have historically become an egoistic hierarchy perpetrated in the name of God. This is indicative of what happens when people get stuck in the mental realm. It is precisely why it is said that the mind makes a great servant but is a terrible master. This section was included to illustrate that egoism in the guise of religion will actually prevent someone from discovering their soul purpose.

Spiritual people practice a series of disciplines that access the unseen domain I refer to as the spiritual realm. The most important spiritual discipline is meditation, but that is a wholly different book. Suffice to say that daily meditation will quiet the mind so your clearly access the spiritual plane. It is critically important to understand that this is the realm in which Soul Purpose resides fully formed. Without accessing the spiritual realm, living one's Soul Purpose is virtually impossible. Thus, it is very important to recognize that without doing the disciplines, it is unlikely for someone to live their Soul Purpose.

The spiritual realm is the place of highest possibility, the mental realm is the middle, and the physical realm is the lowest. People have access to, and always create from, one of three planes of potential. Creating from the physical realm only dictates that we follow basic animal instincts, thus is the most limited realm. Creating from the mental realm exponentially increases results because you have engaged a higher engine, which is the mind, and combined it with the chassis of the body. You are not only working hard (physical) but you are also working smart. Creating form the spiritual realm is a quantum leap unlike any other. It combines all three realms; working hard and smart but driven by the indefatigable power of the God-self. The God-self provides us with an amazing aspiration to succeed because soul purpose is the thing you already most love to do. H2O can be seen as ice, water, or steam depending on the intensity of its molecular speed. Similarly, the human being can be physical, mental, or spiritual depending on the intensity of aspiration to succeed. Careful study of the following chart will illustrate the enormous difference between the potential results in productivity that are possible when creating from the spiritual realm.

| Realm: | Spiritual | Mental | Physical |
|---|---|---|---|
| State: | God-Self | Ego-self | Animal-self |
| Ethic: | Work Mission | Work Smart | Work Hard |
| Essence: | Soul | Mind | Body |
| Process: | Being | Thinking | Doing |
| Business Style: | Creative | Proactive | Reactive |
| Business Model: | Interdependent | Independent | Dependent |

From my research, one year of physical work can create enough value for others to generate twenty thousand dollars of income. One year of working in the mental realm may create enough value for others to earn two hundred thousand dollars of income. One year spent working from the spiritual realm of soul purpose can easily generate two million dollars. Notice the ten times exponential growth that can occur due to the phenomenal leap in power as one transcends from the physical to the mental to the spiritual realm.

To illustrate this point, let's look at someone—a construction worker—who makes his living at the level of the physical realm. The construction worker uses his body to make a living, and while it is honest, honorable work, this career has limited pay and longevity potential. He 'works hard'—but after a while his sore body, lack of creative input, and limited pay make him eventually feel stuck in his body. He is discontented.

Deciding he wants to earn more, he chooses to 'work smart,' and changes careers to one that uses his mind—let's say he chooses a career as a financial planner. He has shifted realms of power from the physical to the mental, into a higher realm of potential in which pay and longevity are greatly increased. Financial planners have been known to work well into their eighties, and some earn millions of dollars a year. He begins studying the stock market and financial trade magazines and enrolls in night school to eventually get a degree as a Certified Financial Planner. Five years later he has a thriving book of business, and looks back in amazement at his old salary of $20,000 a year in construction compared to his current salary of $200,000 a year as a financial planner.

He has used his mind as the way out of the limitations innate to the physical realm, but may have unknowingly adopted the belief that the mind is the way out of every dilemma. While he is earning more, he has reached a false ceiling in his productivity, is overweight, unhappy, and argues with his wife and/or kids. Why? He has now become stuck in his mind. The quandary of the mental realm is that the mind convinces you that it is the pinnacle of human existence. Everyone stuck in the mental realm secretly believes his beliefs are right and superior to others. That which was once the way out, has become the next impediment to be transcended.

One author of this work who has become a close friend now was first a coaching client of mine. He found himself in a dilemma similar to that of the facetious story in the paragraph above. By committedly doing his spiritual disciplines, he created unique products and services that are now generating in excess of two million dollars yearly.

You have the exact same potential, but if you aren't experiencing greater prosperity it is most likely for the following reason. You are a Soul—in a body—who has a reasoning computer called a mind. You are quite probably trapped in the mind, and as such, do not have direct access to your Soul purpose. In fact, so many people are trapped in their mind that they don't even believe the soul exists, much less has a purpose. To begin awakening to your Soul Purpose, start by seeing yourself as the spirit in the body who has a mind, but is not the mind. To verify this as a plausible truth, let's look at what you really are with a greater awareness and clarity, perhaps more so now than ever before.

## WHO ARE YOU REALLY?

Most people consider themselves to be their body—are you the body? The body goes about its business—blood circulation, digestion, heartbeat, neuronal activity, autonomic nervous system functions—without you helping at all. It handles millions of physiological functions every day—fully independent of you whatsoever. Are you thinking about your heartbeat right now, commanding it to happen with each beat? Are you commanding digestion to occur after each meal? Of course not, the body does these things on its own. The more closely you observe, you will begin to see "I have a body, I am not my body." While the body is a great gift, to equate who you are as only the body is to critically limit your potential. Yes, you are to take care of the body as best possible, but the body functions on its own. In fact, it does many things you do not even choose—getting headaches, toothaches, stomach aches, etc.—do you control or choose any of that?

If you were the body you would have much more say over its workings—much like the owner of a company has control over what that company does. He owns it, he controls it. Since you actually have very little control over what the body does, are you the owner of it? Looking more closely, one sees that you actually have only a modicum of control over the body, because you are much more than that. The body is the vehicle and the vessel for who you really are, but quite obviously not you.

Many others believe themselves to primarily be the mind, so let's investigate this idea. An analogy might be useful to illustrate this point more fully. Imagine you're watching TV. When you're bored of watching TV, you—as the owner and controller of the TV—merely choose to turn it off. Can you do that with your mind? NO! Why not? You are not it. Don't the inane ramblings of the mind get boring sometimes too? If you were the mind you would be able to control it and shut it off at will, which you cannot. You didn't start the mind and you can't stop the mind. Thinking is an aspect of consciousness much like getting wet is an aspect of swimming. Thinking happens all by itself; if you exist, its just part of the deal. You can't shut your mind off because you are not it. This understanding is a major turning point in one's soul work. Secondarily, it is important for you to recognize, 'I have a mind, but I am not my mind."

If you are not your body or mind, but instead have a body and a mind, then what are you? You are the life-force energy inside the body, or that which has long been defined as the soul or the spirit. This new belief—I am the Spirit/Soul in the body— will immediately begin freeing you from the clutches of the mental realm. As you do so, your Soul will become more powerful, because this new belief is like spiritual weightlifting. Your spirit, being the greatest part of you, begins to get stronger and stronger the more it is exercised. It only makes sense, doesn't it? Exercise the body and it gets stronger. Exercise the mind and it gets stronger. Exercise the spirit, it gets more powerful, and with discipline, you eventually realize your Soul purpose. It exists fully formed within you, but you may not see it because it is obscured under layers of fear, doubt, and disbelief.

As you gain spiritual strength you'll become aware of the unique combination of inherent talents and abilities that—combined with your life experience—point to it. By living this Soul purpose you will offer the most phenomenal value imaginable to others, and to the world.

*Discovering your Soul purpose and living it every day is the hidden Mission of every person on Earth.*

The Infinite Intelligence programs a unique purpose into the matrix of each person's soul. This unique purpose contains the solution to an existing problem on Earth. This is why you see billions of problems existing on our planet. Even problems have a purpose. They exist so each one of us can discover our own unique Soul Purpose. The unintentional consequence of not discovering Soul Purpose is that the problem your "soul work" can correct goes unsolved. World problems are becoming insurmountable precisely because so few people are aware of, and living, their Soul purpose. As conscious human beings we therefore have a personal and moral responsibility to discover ours. Your soul is now awakening to the truth that you can make this kind of difference.

Notice that we are all born with a distinctive series of interests, passions, and natural talents that exist within—strongly formed in our soul matrix. As an example, Mozart wrote his first symphony at age eight. Anyone can see that this exceptional musical talent was very mature in his soul matrix at birth. He was created to be a great musician, as was Stevie Wonder, Pavarotti, and many others. The talent was innate, they were born with it. So it is with yours. But so many people invalidate their Soul Purpose because it comes so naturally to them. They erroneously assume everyone can do it. Our Soul Purpose is often clearly seen by others close to us even though we unintentionally devalue it. You probably marvel at some unique talent others possess, but they themselves may think nothing of it because it comes so naturally to them. For this reason people often look past the elusive obvious. Since this is your unique Soul Purpose, you may be unintentionally devaluing yourself, while others will see its value and gladly compensate you handsomely for it.

How does Soul purpose tie into greater prosperity? It is important to recall that within a world of seemingly continuous cause and effect, value creation is the cause, and money is the effect. When value is created for another – money, or some other form of abundance, will surely follow back to you. What else could possibly offer the world the greatest value other than living that which you were specifically created for? What else would you also have the most fun doing, knowing you were doing that which you loved to do every single day? What else could you possibly do to have more fun, create more value, and earn the most money from doing than your Soul Purpose? Doesn't that resonate with you? This is the dovetail between spiritual and material wealth.

## ECONOMIC CERTAINTY VIA INTERDEPENDENCY

You increase economic prosperity by creating a team. Interdependency is all about taking a team approach to life, despite the inherent challenges this presents us with. Thus, only the Interdependent business model allows for people to live Soul Purpose and become wealthy in the highest sense of the word. Here are the three basic business models for comparative analysis:

**1. Dependent**—You work for someone else—trade time for money—have little freedom and little control over earnings. Working for long periods of time in this model often results in self-esteem issues.

**2. Independent**—You work for yourself and are self-motivated—trade talent for money—have more freedom and more control over earnings but eventually feel alone, unsupported and suffer having to re-create business on a daily basis.

**3. Interdependent**—You create strategic partnerships with other entrepreneurs—leverage your combined talents and systems to increase money—have greater freedom and control over pay.

Interdependency is more powerful than the other business models for several reasons. First, it empowers everyone in the partnership, even support team members, to experience greater fulfillment because it allows everyone to live their soul purpose. It's obvious that people do better work when they're doing what they love and are rewarded well for doing it. Second, people living their Soul Purpose are driven to persist to a greater degree because they are on a mission. They therefore attract similar people into a soul group.

When I finally committed to living my Soul Purpose, I sought out my highest integrity friends and proposed creating a strategic partnership. I already had an existing client base of people who liked me and trusted me. I noticed that each of my entrepreneur friends also had a valuable service every one of my clients would eventually need. Each one had a great service and system, and also had an existing client base. We created a mutual admiration society in which the total exceeded the sum of the parts. Looking back, the reason it worked so well was that I had chosen the highest integrity people I knew who were already committed to being mission driven.

This model also maximizes the power of leverage. Combining forces with other mission driven beings allows you to leverage:

**1. Other People's Experience**—Everyone in our network knew something about business that I previously didn't know, that they shared with me, and from which I benefited.

**2. Other People's Money**—By combining financial resources we were able to do projects any one of us could not have afforded to do alone.

**3. Other People's Ideas**—Every team member was creative in slightly different ways—so they each brought unique ideas about advertising, marketing, research, and a myriad number of other crucial business topics.

**4. Other People's Time**—They were willing to cover for me admirably when I was away on vacation, out sick, or taking a free day.

**5. Other People's Energy**—They picked me up and inspired me when I was down—as I did for them—and we gladly allowed each other to ride the others' coattails when necessary.

**6. Other People's Clients**—We created an internal switch for referring business to each other when the need arose—which it somehow did more often, once we made that commitment.

The father of what is now modern architecture was the ancient Greek engineer Archimedes, who said, "Give me a lever long enough, and a place to stand, and I'll move the world." He was referring to the power of leverage to create greater success momentum.

I have heard many entrepreneurs tell me they tried this approach, but that it didn't work for them. After doing an organizational x-ray of their company, I almost always discovered the same reason it hadn't worked. The hard truth was that they were not behaving as mission driven beings, regardless of what they were outwardly saying. Because of ego delusion they were operating from fear, desire, or pride, therefore drawing the same kind of partners to them. Of course this kind of selfish partnership cannot possibly prosper on a consistent basis. Negativity caused their team to crumble, as it always does, and rightfully so.

Other so-called networks of people who are not mission driven invariably collapse. Here are some examples of how and why this may occur. The examples shown below include six-team members in each strategic partnership. A mathematics equation follows each example to give an economics example of the direct proportion in value created to dollars earned.

Fear-Driven network: Team members talk about success but no one believes in themselves, much less each other—so no referrals, time, energy, money or any other resources are shared. With fear at their core, they drain each other instead of inspiring each other. This has the opposite desired effect of the original purpose, and energy is subtracted causing the ego-self to be reinforced. Every time the idea of networking or strategic partnerships arises in the future each former member says, "I tried it but it doesn't work."

Economics principle of Subtraction. The team members, there are six of them in this example, actually subtract energy from each other:

1—1—1—1—1—1 =—$60,000 (Fear subtracts group energy—negative paradigm is reinforced—money invested is gone when the group disbands or company goes bankrupt)

Pride-driven network: These networks are often populated by fairly successful earners who are willing to try a new idea only for the sake of money, but lack understanding of the true principles required to succeed using interdependency.

Pride causes this team to view money as the asset—instead of seeing that the true asset is people. This blinds each member to the concept that creating value first for others will eventually result in more money. This network contains people who want to receive the benefits of greater business, without the willingness to give referrals to the right strategic partner. These men are so habitually committed to their own success first and foremost (independent), that they developed the habit of rarely giving referrals.

Dollars may be made in the short-term because of the initial energy boost that occurs by putting moneymakers together, but often fizzles quickly because of violation of the following interdependent success principle. Because of a lack of understanding the Law of Vibration and Attraction, they fail to realize that the more they give to each other, the more opportunity they will receive from each other.

### Economics principle of Addition

1 + 1 + 1 + 1 + 1 + 1 = \$60,000 (A little extra money but no velocity of value—hence, the alliance is eventually viewed as not worth it and the group disbands.)

Mission-driven network: By living your soul purpose mission, you attract others with impeccable integrity who are also committed to being mission-driven. By becoming the right partner, you draw more of the right partners. This synergistic partnership model turns clients into partners and partners into clients.

Everyone in our network realizes the others have something great, and utilize each other's business processes and products. This book is evidence of this practice. We give each other our own business, and receive value from each other's great services and products. Because we personally experience the direct value each member offers, we want to refer each team member to all family and friends. Years ago as we began doing this, we collectively experienced something astounding. By giving more referrals, we began to receive more great referrals from all over the country.

You will experience the same. By giving more business you receive more great business. This behavior is so valuable to mission-driven professionals that they want to reciprocate and send value back to you. It becomes a competition to see who can create the most value for each other—not the least. Because of the exponential multiplication of power that happens at this level of understanding and operating, you increase the velocity of value.

### Economics principle of Multiplication

$6^2$ = 6 x 6 = \$360,000 (velocity of value exponentially multiplies group energy and income).

You can easily see from these hypothetical examples that potential results expand exponentially when one accesses the spiritual realm and lives soul purpose.

You are so very great. You have so much to bring to the world, yet you may be settling for far less. This is because ninety-nine percent of people in the world do not live Soul Purpose, so there seems to be strength in numbers. It will appear to be daring, even risky, to seek and live your Soul Purpose. The opposite is true—not daring to live it is the greatest risk you could ever take. Please dare to believe in yourself—we do.

\* If you would like more information about these unique concepts, you can email Steve at prosperitysteve@gmail.com or call 1 (800) 452-7203. You can also visit www.prosperityparadigm.com on the web.

# CHAPTER 4

# JASON BYRNE
Home Trust, Inc.

*Jason Byrne's life passion is to help others discover and grow their Soul Purpose™ and achieve Economic Freedom through real estate.*

*While in high school, in a national magazine sales contest, he was the #1 salesperson in the nation. While earning his degree in Finance from the University of Colorado at Boulder he was a key player in a successful high tech start-up. From there he became Chief Operating Officer of 15 quick service restaurants with 240 associates – at age 25.*

*By 2001 the allure of real estate was inescapable, and he and his wife Hope founded HomeTrust™. Initially buying, renovating, and selling homes, HomeTrust™ has since spawned five other real estate businesses. The most notable of which is The Fresh Start System by HomeTrust™, whose mission is To Stop Foreclosure, One Family At a Time. As Chairman of The Fresh Start System™, Jason leads the Company's marketing, does frequent seminars and radio appearances, and develops strategic partnerships and spin off businesses.*

*Jason owns real estate in multiple states, and his companies act as principals in the sale of over 150 single family homes per year. He is the creator of The Renter's Escape Plan™, The Problem House Solution™, and The Credit Restoration Machine™. He is also on the Board of Advisors of the HomeTrust Solutions Center, Inc., a 501(c)3 non-profit that provides home retention and loss mitigation services to borrowers and lenders by offering innovative alternatives to home foreclosure.*

*Jason and Garrett Gunderson share a passion for helping others discover, grow, and live their Soul PurposeTM while achieving Economic Freedom. This passion has spawned several businesses including The Business BluePrint™.*

*Jason lives at the foot of the Rockies in Boulder, Colorado, with wife Hope and their three grade school aged children. Outside of work Jason's passions are adventurous travel with Hope and the kids, powder skiing, and cycling in the mountains.*

*For more information visit www.hometrustinfo.com. Jason can be reached at: jbyrne@hometrustinfo.com or 800-400-5206.*

## DISCONTENT: THE JET FUEL FOR CHANGE

t was 2AM on December 28, 2005 and I was on the bathroom floor puking my guts out. I was terrified. I had just absorbed the truth: the real state of my failing company and it was brutal. I panicked. I could feel the rhythmic pounding of blood flowing through my head – pounding so hard I feared for my life. Should I call an ambulance? What was happening? This was extreme emotional distress causing intense physical pain.

What I was acknowledging was a deep knowing that my business in 2005 was not working. Seriously not working. The loss was well into six figures. My problem? I was functioning as a solo entrepreneur. I didn't understand how to engage the productive ability of my Soul Purpose because I did not know about it. I had not engaged the Soul Purposes of others. And my bank account showed it.

In my ignorance of Soul Purpose and its undiscovered potential in my life I was stuck. In my arrogance and desire to avoid unpleasant work, I had ramped up the operations and fixed expenses of my real estate development business, and my revenue and profit weren't enough to justify me paying others to do the work I didn't want to do. Instead of understanding and engaging other people's Soul Purpose and aligning their self-interest with mine, I threw money at people and asked them to perform work that was not in their Soul Purpose. I hired people indiscriminately. Unfortunately, I avoided accepting this and faced it much later than I could have. When the facts could be avoided no longer I had to admit things were pretty dark. That December 28, 2005, I was making decisions that were making me sick. Literally.

I saw the potential that everything I had been working for might vanish. If we couldn't be profitable and keep the business going then all of the ideas, the vision, the processes I had worked so hard to achieve would go down the drain. No wonder I was freaking out. I would have to face everyone who said I'd never make it as an entrepreneur and call myself a failure I had set off on the journey of work and life thinking only of myself. Big mistake.

I was, as Strategic Coach founder Dan Sullivan would say, a Rugged Individualist. Sitting alone in my underwear in my basement office, creating all these ideas that were going to change the world, was fun for a couple of years. Then I realized my ideas were just ideas – they were not being executed and creating value out in the world. Darn it! I'm just sitting here alone – again – dreaming. There was not enough production taking place, no Soul Purpose creating value in the world, no Soul Purpose Teams. It was just me, and I was not creating value in the marketplace.

## GARRETT GUNDERSON AND LES MCGUIRE

Garrett, Les, and I had been Strategic Coach classmates since January of 2004. I had seen their business and financial lives expand VERY quickly. I was still in the Consumer Condition, and I wanted what they had, but didn't know how to get it. In October 2005 I heard Les say, "I just bought a $185,000 Mercedes, and I now have more portfolio income than I used to have active income." My Consumer antennae went up, and I asked what he was doing to make this happen. Garrett responded, "We're doing a Curriculum For Wealth Symposium tomorrow in Colorado, an hour from your house. You should come. We'll tell you what we're doing."

And they did. My mind was blown that day learning from Garrett and Les. I understood Soul Purpose. I understood how to put Soul Purpose into production. I understood Dollars Follow Value. I understood creating value for others first, before thinking of what was in it for me, was in fact the highest expression of my self-interest. I understood why I had never been a good business partner and how to change it. In short, this day profoundly altered the drift of my life.

Until that point I knew I was working hard and smart. I just wasn't putting people first, and I wasn't honoring Soul Purpose. I was more interested in creating value for myself than others. I wanted success first. But finally I understood there is another component to this. I identified how a specific Soul Purpose creates value, for who it creates value, and what support people are required on the Soul Purpose Team to achieve the result of value creation. Soul Purpose, delivered with PASSION and EACH of those components has led to financial abundance for my family and my partners.

## IDENTIFICATION OF MY SOUL PURPOSE

I first identify my Soul Purpose with a personal energy evaluation. After I do a task, regardless of the quantity of time spent, how do I feel? Do I feel like I have more energy or less energy?

The energy I get from working in my Soul Purpose is a physical energy. I can walk out of a Soul Purpose activity I've been doing for an hour or 12 hours, and I have so much physical energy I want to go out and go for a bicycle ride in the mountains or go to the park with the kids. I'm just filled with physical energy. It springs from deep within me.

Part of my personal Soul Purpose is to aggressively and systematically organize ideas and methodologies into Soul Purpose Process growth vehicles that can be scaled into big "value creation first, dollars second" opportunities which create abundance and ever increasing Freedom for my family, our partners, associates, and our clients. When I am doing that I get tremendous energy. Another part is to share my story about Soul Purpose and how it led to the creation of all these great companies I work on with my partners.

Attempting to do almost anything manual is so draining for me, it's almost comical. For example, I was trading out our car's bike rack for the ski rack, and my kids could see my incompetence and suggested I hire someone to help. I just sat there and smiled and started laughing because here's an example of non-Soul Purpose, an activity that took much too long, drained energy, and was frustrating. I felt an absolute lack of passion, and no matter how long I spent doing manual activity like that I would probably never get better because I have no desire at all to get better. That's non-Soul Purpose.

Your Soul Purpose might be in business, or it might be in some form of social work or family emphasis. It doesn't have to be about business or making money. But it does have to be about creating value because, by definition, when you operate in your Soul Purpose, you create more value than you consume. Like me, you will naturally be in the Prosperity Paradigm (see www.TheProsperityParadigm.com for more details) when you recognize and act in your Soul Purpose.

I love doing my Soul Purpose activities so much I would do them even if I weren't getting paid. I do it for the love and the joy of it and, by definition, I create more value than I take. I am "genius" in my Soul Purpose, like everyone else is in theirs, and I just want to keep producing.

The genius or the expert piece of Soul Purpose, in my experience, is that my Soul Purpose comes so easily to me that it's literally like child's play; that's how I actually describe it. That might be offensive to some people, but I really describe it as child's play. It's just fun, because it comes so easily to me. My Soul Purpose work takes so little effort and energy from me, and I feel better after doing the project.

## SOUL PURPOSE IN ACTION

As an example, going back to value first and dollars will follow, last year I started making regular trips from my home in Boulder, Colorado to Salt Lake City – at my expense and without immediate monetary compensation. I was so passionate about what Garrett Gunderson and his partners were doing that I wanted to be involved. So I simply showed up. It started as a shadowing day that evolved into Garrett and myself now being partners in six businesses.

I started applying my Soul Purpose to the benefit of Garrett's business, and Garrett immediately recognized how I created value and asked me to do more and more of it. That's how Producers create win-wins through Soul Purpose application and Soul Purpose Teams. It's effortless. And Dollars Always Follow Value. So now, in addition to applying my Soul Purpose and building Soul Purpose Teams to make our original real estate company a success, and forming four other high value businesses with great partners in Denver, I have expanded my Soul Purpose value creation to Garrett and Salt Lake City. And that's just the beginning.

People ask me, "My gosh! How can you do that? How can you create all these businesses? How can you have all these partnerships? How do you keep it all straight in your head? How can you come up with all these ideas? How can you come up with these Soul Purpose Processes? How can you create these Soul Purpose Teams? How can you put these management models into place? How can you create this intellectual capital? How can you do all this stuff?"

And I just shrug my shoulders and say, "It just comes so easily to me." THAT, ladies and gentlemen, is Soul Purpose in ACTION…

This really goes hand in hand with the genius piece. Going back three years, I spent 5% of my time in my Soul Purpose, but rarely put the fruits into production. A year ago I spent maybe 20% of my time in my Soul Purpose. And frankly I wasn't all that happy or successful.

Today I spend about 50% of my time in my Soul Purpose, and the acceleration that has occurred in my life in terms of happiness, value creation, economic impact, and the currency I'm able to create for those around me and my family has been absolutely tremendous. I can't wait to see what life is like when I am able to spend 90% of my time on my Soul Purpose! I'll be there soon.

Soul Purpose action with intent creates abundance, and abundance creates better and larger Soul Purpose Teams. As my life becomes more financially abundant, I am able to apply those resources towards other people who can take non-Soul Purpose activities away from me. Then I can just spend more and more time on my Soul Purpose. When there's a work situation where I leave drained of energy, I find someone who gets energy from that task, who is in their Soul Purpose in that role, and find a way for them to do that role instead of me. Understand, this is a gradual process, it doesn't happen overnight, although it has happened quickly for me.

When I spend more time on my Soul Purpose I keep getting better. When I keep getting better there are more business models, better ideas, higher quality products, superior intellectual capital, greater value creation, happier clients, better paid partners. It's exponential growth. It is not linear. And I love exponential growth.

## SOUL PURPOSE TEAMS AND INTERDEPENDENCE

I understand the importance of having people around me who have Soul Purpose where I do not. I create the exchange where I pay them for the value they provide. They feel great about this because they're getting currency for their effort, and I get to spend more time in my Soul Purpose. This enhances my enjoyment of life and my health and wealth and happiness. It makes the world go round. 2005 was before we had Soul Purpose Teams. I had limited value creation, and my bank account reflected that fact.

Now I understand that I am certainly increasing my cash outflow when I engage someone else for his or her Soul Purpose contribution. I'm also dramatically increasing my productivity. I'm helping them because they have an ability then to get paid for their Soul Purpose and to spend more time in their Soul Purpose.

This is a great example of how my Soul Purpose is not really about real estate. It's about creating powerful Soul Purpose Teams that deliver tremendous value and unique experiences to our clients. Part of this includes growing companies, which often requires helping people discover their Soul Purpose in every aspect of their life and helping them get employed or engaged in their Soul Purpose. When we have a person accountable for each part of our Soul Purpose Processes, and they are operating in their Soul Purpose, the results we achieve are tremendous. Our associates love their work, they are getting energy from it, they are geniuses, and they are passionate.

When our associate's job is within their Soul Purpose they are joyful. When they're joyful they do a wonderful job, they're more productive because they're working faster, they're creating more value for the client which creates more value for the firm which creates more currency to go around. That is how we have increased our financial abundance.

In addition to creating financial abundance, I am a better person when we have Soul Purpose Teams in action. Specifically I have more energy for the people and activities that matter to me. That makes me happy. I am successfully doing the things I excel at and enjoy, I feel great when I am creating value for others and myself, and I can be calm, centered and present in my life.

To me, interdependence is building Soul Purpose Teams with equity partners. In our eleven businesses, we have partners in ten. Our original business, the one that had me puking, is now healthy, and it's the only business where we don't have partners. The ten others have all been formed since I discovered my Soul Purpose.

I am so grateful to each of my partners, because their Soul Purposes compliment my Soul Purpose so well. My Soul Purpose includes vision, planning, building high-level relationships, and seeing Soul Purpose Processes from a high level. It does not include daily operations, daily sales activities, or managing technology projects. My partners abundantly bring these skills to the table, I bring mine, and together—in interdependence—we are moving mountains.

The key to interdependence's success, in my experience, is creating a win for my partners before I think about creating a win for me. Ironically, I have discovered that is the best way to serve my self-interest. Yes, our partnerships encounter obstacles. We have disagreements, and we have times when we're not particularly happy with each other. But each of my partners live in the Prosperity Paradigm, each of them are Producers, and therefore we are able to work through the rough spots. The benefits dramatically outweigh the costs.

## WHERE SOUL PURPOSE HAS BROUGHT ME TODAY

Today I work in stark contrast to the Rugged Individualist alone in my basement. My main office is in the Denver Tech Center on the 5th floor - facing west to the mountains I love, which is a great view from our balcony. Successful partners surround me, and we are all operating in our Soul Purposes as Soul Purpose Teams. Sure, we each do things we dislike sometimes, but we constantly strive to decrease those tasks for each other. It is fun and it feels great to have contributed to the success of each of these individuals and to be creating amazing value and experiences for our clients. I am grateful for the opportunity to use my gifts to help others and to help my family.

The financial abundance that is coming into my life, as a byproduct of focusing on my Soul Purpose and building Soul Purpose Teams in interdependency, is greater than I had ever envisioned. That's really saying something, because I have always been a dreamer who thinks big.

## ONE YEAR LATER, AND 180 DEGREES DIFFERENT

It was 11PM on December 31, 2006 and I was terrified. One year since the, ahem, puking incident. My heart was pounding again. I had just faced the fact that I was perched at the top of my friend's sledding hill on a toboggan with Hope and our 3 kids, and I felt the exhilaration and terror of flying down the hill, feeling an out-of-control giddiness.

And in that moment I felt peace. The kind of peace that only comes with financial abundance and a purpose in life. I had found mine and it was delightful. Here's to you finding yours.

# CHAPTER 5

# KIM BUTLER
## Partners For Prosperity, Inc.

*Kim has been a highly successful leader in the field of financial services since 1988. She first learned the value of work growing up on a farm in Oregon. In fact, Kim milked cows to put herself through private college. Whatever the circumstance, Kim has a gift for creating alternative ways to succeed. She is now a Kolbe Certified consultant, a Certified Financial Planner, and a Coach for the Strategic Coach Program.*

*Kim is also the founder of The P4P Process, which offers non-traditional financial planning for the entrepreneurial mind with a mission statement to create financial confidence and guide clients toward their maximum wealth. Kim is able to use her ability to spot relevant patterns and issues to help her clients understand and utilize the velocity of money, the multiplier effect, lost opportunity cost and create turbo-charged strategies for creating what they want in life.*

*When Kim isn't busy strategizing with her clients, she puts her energy and skillful stamina to good use by enjoying time with her family, volunteering with animal charities, hiking, rollerblading, working on husband Todd Langford's alpaca farm and reading.*

*To receive information on how to maximize your wealth, contact the number below.*

**Partners For Prosperity, Inc.**

*4110 North Street • Nachodoches TX 75965*

*1(877)889-3981 • email: p4pinfo@p4pemail.com • www.Partners4Prosperity.com*

## VISIONEERING

**M**y soul purpose is what I call visioneering, which guides all the players towards and end goal while ensuring that everyone grows along the way. Simply put, I love to help others grow and I believe in and practice working in my Soul Purpose every day. I feel strongly that if I'm not growing, I'm dying. I've been told I'm effective at helping change the way others think of themselves while inspiring them to change both their perceptions and actions. I fully believe and have experienced that individuals can get paid to do what they love to do. They just have to do it in a way that provides value to others.

Part of living Soul Purpose is using your personal talents to benefit others. Just recently there were 2 different instances when a "tough phone call" had to be made. I volunteered to do it because being willing to confront issues head on is a talent God gave me and so I willingly lend it to others when it helps our whole team. Obviously there are times when another person has to deal with his or her own issues but if it's a team issue, I'm happy to tackle it if its something I excel at. When I'm working on a problem, my juices are flowing, I'm engaged, operating from my Soul Purpose, which causes others and myself to stretch and grow. In this example I could literally see (visualize) the end result we wanted. That is what enables me to move past any fear or concern, such as stepping on toes, and take appropriate action.

## DISCOVERING SOUL PURPOSE

I've been attending The Strategic Coach® Program in Chicago since 1995, and they have their own conceptual framework and term for Soul Purpose, and it's a constant focus of the Program. They introduced me to the Kolbe® profile and the Strengths Finder™ profile which greatly helped me to discover my existing set of talents. Then they helped me systematically eliminate activities that didn't support my Soul Purpose. If you're interested in finding out more about his, just visit www.strategiccoach.com and purchase their Knowledge Product called Unique Ability®: Creating the Life You Want and follow its guidance. I personally found it to be very helpful in gaining insights into what was, and what wasn't, a part of my individual Soul Purpose.

Discovering your Soul Purpose takes self-knowledge, trial and error and is an ongoing effort of refinement, ideally for the rest of your life. My teammate Rodney Stockton and I are currently helping my sister Tammi Brannan through this discovery process. I've been helping her question herself deeply about what is important to her. Watching this process is like watching a time-lapse photo as it unfolds before your very eyes. It's joy-filled work and hugely rewarding. If our world supported each person following their Soul Purpose there would be no unemployment and no such thing as mid-life crisis.

## LIVING SOUL PURPOSE

Is it always easy for me to follow my Soul Purpose? Yes and No. Sometimes one is obligated to activities, yet they aren't committed to them. However, a conscientious human being will want to finish what they started.

Knowing oneself is not an easy task. Sometimes I still get involved with non-Soul Purpose areas and then have to slowly get back out of it. I liken it to the dog with the zap collar inside the invisible fence. The better I stay inside my fence of Soul Purpose, the better off my days are! But it does get much easier with practice. Back when I was less sure of my Soul Purpose I hung in there, knowing what my Soul Purpose had in store for me if I kept going. Knowing that a person can do anything for a short period of time, I was able to persevere through non-Soul Purpose activities. However, seeing the light at the end of the tunnel enabled me to want to follow my Soul Purpose even more. What can you learn? That following your Soul Purpose can be difficult but it's totally worth it! Find a way to follow it at least a little bit every day until you get to a place where you are following it at least 80% of the time.

## OVERCOMING DOUBT

When I first started living in my Soul Purpose, as in making sure I was spending most of my time on activities that energized me, there were many doubters. My family, friends and work associates all questioned the validity of actually being able to pull that off. I'm glad I stuck with it and continue to do so as it makes life so much more fun. It may be going "against" the grain of society but going "with" it led me to live a life of frustration, and I don't care to continue down that road. I've also seen the wonderful things that come from living Soul Purpose in the lives of my work associates. Bottom line, the difficulty of following Soul Purpose is far out-weighed by all of the amazing benefits.

By living my Soul Purpose I have also brought much more happiness and joy into the lives of others. My husband Todd Langford taught me the distinction between happiness and joy. Joy can exist regardless of outside circumstances, and we strive to live joyfully daily.  Fulfillment at work became the norm because it became okay to not be good at certain things. Again from The Strategic Coach® I learned that building a Unique Ability® Team enabled me to focus on improving my strengths and those strengths of others instead of trying to develop my own, or others, weaknesses. Surrounding myself with activities that support my Soul Purpose makes life more fun. Even better, surrounding myself with other people also working in their Soul Purpose elevates life even further. Kathy Kolbe's definition of success is the freedom to be you.  Living my Soul Purpose is living that self and being free to be me, and being appreciated for that, loved because of it, and encouraged to do more of it.

My advice is to keep striving to live your life the way you want to and let others live theirs the way they want to.  Appreciate differences! I remember early in my life hearing from a friend Heidi Christianson that she liked to do craft work. I thought she was crazy.  Now I've learned how incredibly diverse each of us are and how important to our world that is. I've had to learn how to appreciate differences and by doing so, Heidi has helped my kids Robert and Kaylea with a part of them (their artistic side) that I couldn't have helped with. My new mom, Melissa Hays has continued this effort. By proactively being grateful to Heidi and Melissa and acknowledging their skills in this area, supporting their ability to demonstrate their Soul Purpose, my kids got some unique education, and I improved as well.

## A SOUL PURPOSE FOR EVERYONE

A big "Ah-ha" moment for me was realizing that there were people who's Soul Purpose in life is to do things I didn't like to do, just like my Soul Purpose is on other's "don't like" list. That was a huge mental paradigm shift because we get so inside ourselves, we think everyone sees the world the way we do. Thank goodness they don't! I still have to remind myself of this very often.  There really are people who love to (fill in the blank); even if that is something I might dread doing. How wonderful it is that God made us all so different! If you were to make a list of your 3 most despised activities, I'm confident you could find someone somewhere who would trade you those for something on their list! Even though I had my first career in a bank, I didn't like to balance checkbooks and keep track of money on a daily basis. I thought it was something I was just going to have to toughen up and do anyway. Then I met Carrie. She loves detail, specificity, accounting programs and cents (no wonder my check book never balanced, I rounded everything off!) And she was willing to be paid to do work she loved to do so I could do something else. What a concept!

Some people wonder how they can better live their Soul Purpose and how to make the difficult decisions that may arise. Personally, I try to listen to the situation, trying hard to hear it clearly and not jump to conclusions (this is hard for me to do). Then I pray, quietly, listening for God's direction. Then I follow my instincts and act quickly (this is easy for me, it fits my style, I'm not suggesting it for everyone since all our instincts are different). But basically, I think more of us need to learn to trust our instincts more often and more quickly. It does take practice. Be humble.

Sometimes to be successful, we have to let others be right. On example of this is that our firm had a new receptionist that I really liked yet others were seeing major problems with her. One day while I was out of town the situation blew up due to some errors on her part. I spoke with 4 different people and heard their side before calling her to hear hers. Then I prayed to God to help us make this a win-win for everyone. After speaking again to P4P partner, John Baker, his suggestion was to let her go and my gut reaction was to agree, even though I didn't necessarily want to see her go. In this case someone else was right. Admitting that I was wrong, and the team was right, is hard but always gets you further ahead faster.

To stay motivated you have to understand what inspires you. For me, I get energy when I see results, growth, new ideas, and technological capability that transform lives. These things inspire me to do more. I like to be growing in all areas of my life all the time. I'm inspired when I'm stretched. I'm inspired when I can move quickly and get good results fast. Answering the question of what inspires you isn't always easy, but if you identify a few things and then go seek them out, you can live a Soul-Purposed life. This is an ongoing challenge, not a one-time event.

Since I've learned to pay attention to how I'm physically feeling when I'm doing something, I know when I'm energized. For example, when I'm helping someone make a paradigm shift I get a lot of energy, so I know that I should keep doing that type of activity. I've learned that when I feel physically asleep I should find a way to enable someone else who's Soul Purpose is more aligned with the activity to do that work. Teammate Ron Weeks is our persistently patient practitioner. I'm so grateful we have him on the P4P team, as there are clients who desire his pace and "stick-to-it-tive-ness".  That is why our firm works as a team, enabling each of us to more closely align with Soul Purpose.

People ask me, why do you do what you do? I tell that that it's so I can keep growing, and help others grow which enables me to grow more and also energizes me. I like changing people's minds, opening them up to new ideas or paradigm shifts. I like challenges and confronting them head on.  Just keep asking yourself this question: "Am I doing the best thing for all concerned right now?"  It will help you maintain momentum through your day and it will help you stay on track.

## A CHANGING PERSPECTIVE

Society is slowing starting to understand the overall concept of Soul Purpose, mostly due to the innovation of successful people who aren't afraid of doing things outside of the mold. When Robert and Kim Kiyosaki were referred to us from another real estate oriented client, they listened to our "non-traditional" philosophy during our first conversation with smiles on their faces. This was unusual to me, because at that time during the late 90's most clients had to be convinced that traditional financial planning was keeping their wealth minimized. The Kiyosakis were agreeing with everything I was saying, instead of arguing with it. Robert was just putting the finishing touches on his first book, Rich Dad, Poor Dad and his breakthrough learning game Cashflow 101 ®. Later they toured the country promoting his story as a learning tool for others, he helped us expand our practice from its Arizona base. People who are ready to live their Soul Purpose can greatly expand the lives of others. If you're ready to live Soul Purpose, you will eventually find yourself mentoring and inspiring others in some way. It's inevitable!

For me, I just love seeing the progress people can make. I love helping them increase their confidence, and watching the results that come about that make major changes in their lives, and the lives of others. Being in a position where I can gently encourage a change in thinking, then in acting is part of living my Soul Purpose. I also believe it's important to have a whole team around you that is also living their Soul Purpose. When you share the fame, profit, progress, results and credit and you can accomplish anything.

In the beginning as an entrepreneur, I took the obvious step of hiring an assistant to help me with the things I wasn't as good at that directly affected our business. Then I realized that an assistant couldn't be good at everything either, so we broke the job down and outsourced the parts she didn't want to do. This can be done at any level, even within a family, by trading jobs one likes for another's dislikes and its extremely effective and freeing. This applies to every aspect of life

## THE SOUL PURPOSE PROCESS

Sometimes, taking time off from work and life in some form enables thinking about Soul Purpose in a way that is hard to do when you are in work and life. During college I was interested in law, so I started on an English degree. As I progressed and got to know more about myself I took more business classes, as they held my interest, and I could see how I might apply the knowledge. During my junior year I interned with a law firm for a quarter and learned so much. One thing in particular was that I didn't appreciate the thinking that many lawyers have to operate with. That quarter I lived with Amanda Price who worked at a bank. We talked about all the things she was doing and I really enjoyed hearing about her work. My senior year I interned with a temporary agency placing workers and got to vicariously experience many different businesses, which enabled me to decide that banking was the best match.

After graduating, for the next 3 years I worked in the bank's branch system, in their loan department and a little in the trust department. During that time a banking client, Nate Sachs, told me I would be good at selling life insurance and mutual funds and I was ready for growth so I took a leap of faith and left the bank. I spent 2 months interviewing and thinking about what I wanted to do. This time of Soul Purpose searching was scary yet valuable. It led me to start studying for my CFP® (Certified Financial Planner) designation while I obtained all the appropriate licenses and made my living selling financial products in what we now call "traditional financial planning" over the next 5 years. At that point I was ready for new growth and started searching for a better way to help our clients more truthfully, because I became aware that every financial plan was filled with assumptions that would never come true.

Then came along another stepping-stone towards understanding my Soul Purpose. Our first baby Robert had just been born, I took 6 weeks off to be at home with him and to study a non-traditional financial planning system. A year later our daughter Kaylea was born and I got some further Soul Purpose thinking time since I wanted to give her the same 6 weeks of special attention. Both times I was prepared for the "mommy bug" to hit me but it did not, so I happily went back to work full time allowing for our nanny June to use her Soul Purpose in caring for our babies and later Cherry Hughes as they became toddlers. I love my children, and I love being their mother, but not everyone has the same aptitude and talents. By employing an individual who's Soul Purpose is to work with and care for children, I was able to more fully live my Soul Purpose, as well.

## WHAT OUR SOUL PURPOSE TEAM OFFERS

As always, teamwork is the only way to go. In my firm, our mission is to "educate council and guide our clients toward the use of their maximum wealth". The vision we operate under is "to increase your financial confidence." We work in about 40 states; so all our educating is done over the phone and the web so clients can learn by both hearing and seeing. I'm so grateful for our current team of John Baker, Todd Langford, Rodney Stockton, Ron Weeks, Theresa Sheridan and Derek Diaz as we all work together to help our clients towards the use of their maximum wealth.

In 2003 Todd Langford and John Baker had been spending their time traveling across the country teaching other "non-traditional" financial planners. They were tired of the travel and ready for a change so we decided to work together since we all shared the same philosophy. It didn't matter that they lived in a small town in Texas since our clients were all over the place anyway. Creating a sustainable partnership is a tough thing in today's world where people are quick to criticize and seek greener pastures elsewhere, rarely looking at themselves as a possible source of the problem. Our partnership has succeeded because we put our egos aside, try hard to listen to one another, and all work for the common good of our clients. In 2005, Todd and I got married which has added additional challenges, yet even further solidified our commitment to P4P. The process we developed is called The Wealth Capitalization

System™ and it has 5 steps that help our clients increase their financial confidence. First is Discovery. Second is Benchmark. Third is Strategy. Fourth is Synopsis. Fifth is Expander. (*More information is available at www.partners4prosperity.com*)

We help people with DISCOVERY. Beginning with a "clarity" session where we walk you through a series of questions that 1) help you get clear about what it will take to help you be financially confident and 2) enable us to be clear about each of your financial pieces that make up your economy or circle of wealth, which basically asks "Would you like to see how to expand your economy or circle of wealth without increasing risk?

**BENCHMARK**: an "understanding" session where we show you The Prosperity Confidence Circle ™ which will give you an understanding about the action steps you will want to take to reduce transferred costs and begin to grow your economy or circle of wealth more efficiently…Would you like to eliminate opportunity cost and be confident you understand how to make your money work harder?

**STRATEGY**: an "action" session that identifies the products you'll want to BUY and the strategies you'll want to USE to get results…Would you like to see how to expand your economy or circle of wealth without increasing risk?

**SYNOPSIS**: an "optimization" session that enables you to see the results of your actions and be confident that you are taking the right steps…Would you like to see what the possibilities are now?

**EXPANDER**: an ongoing "confidence" session where you can put all your information in a Living Balance Sheet where it is automatically updated and available to you 24/7 in a secure spot on the web, protectively stored and ready to facilitate discussion, decision making, protection and action…Would you like to have the tools to feel more confident about on-going financial decision making and growth?

In addition we focus on 2 unique areas: how to use your life insurance death benefit while you are living and how to get one dollar to do more than one job using velocity of money methods. We have also licensed Freedom FastTrack™ to add to our offerings for our clients. Its 7 steps are as follows:

**Freedom FastTrack**

**THE PATH** – Paving your road to prosperity. Getting clear that creating wealth in your life is done by maximizing the value you produce for others. Exploring the difference between producers and consumers. Covering the value provided and tuition received for the 7 stages of Financial Freedom FastTrack™. Would you like to be clear on what Freedom means to me?

**THE SOUL PURPOSE ACTIVATOR** - Cultivating the wealth within you. Walking you through a series of questions designed to help you identify and activate your soul purpose. Identifying the future growth that will happen in your life, financially and in your human life value. Would you like to identify both Seen and Unseen resources?

**THE CASTLE AND MOAT BLUEPRINT** – A landscape of your life. Understanding that individual components must coordinate together to both build and protect. Analyzing current financial and Human Life value resources and putting them to better use, both for today and in the future. Would you like to convert Potential into Production?

**THE PROTECTION / PRODUCTION CONTINUUM** – Maximizing, leveraging and protecting human life value. Learning that all things, financial and otherwise produce better once they are fully protected. Discovering that freedom comes from having both and aligning your actions with your improved knowledge about timeless economic principles will get you results. Would you like to know and Work with these principles?

**THE ABUNDANCE ACCELERATOR** – A macro economic advantage. Putting all the pieces together. Building up from the expertise of the Accredited Network of Advisors available to you while working on your financial blue print. Would you like to manage financial risk to near zero?

**THE STATE OF WEALTH** - From philosophy to prosperity. Reviewing all the steps taken, items learned, actions completed, progress made. Designating a follow up process so additional opportunities are captured properly. Expanding the possibilities outward to include others so you are not on this path alone. Would you like to increase your Human Life Value and Expand your wealth creation capability?

**THE EXCELLENCE ETHIC** – A producer's standard. Introducing the Five Pillars of Human Life Value and how freedom is available in all areas through continued study and growth. Discussing how your own Soul Purpose could play a role in expanding these opportunities. Which path will you choose…same Old path or New path?

David Sloan has worked with us for about 5 years. Thankfully when he started working with us, he had already done a good job in protecting his Human Life Value with disability and life insurance. We expanded upon that base and helped him implement a few strategies based on the economic principles we teach. In speaking with him recently, he shared that everything we'd suggested he BUY and DO was really starting to work—even though it went against the grain of what many others had suggested. He identified it all started with a change in this thinking. We were both grateful he'd made the progress he had both personally and financially. David's medical condition has caused him to use both his disability insurance and his waiver of premium on his life insurance. However, since he has a Producer attitude, he has not stopped creating. The "self-completion" portion of his finances enables him to share with his community and his family and he loves his life.

The various processes we've offered our clients have always been fully supported by excellent people that sometimes do more to help our clients than even the partners do. Currently Theresa Sheridan and Derek Diaz play this role, and were both involved in helping recently when we were out of town. Clients need answers and they don't usually care where the answer comes from as long as they're correct. Theresa and Derek wear all hats when the partners are away and their use of their own Soul Purpose activities enables them to spread their wings wide so when we return, there is not a backload of work.

## SOUL PURPOSE & THE ACCREDITED NETWORK

I've been asked about my experience with the Accredited Network. For me, being with a group of like-minded, growth oriented, future focused principle-based entrepreneurs is a joy. It's like a family office with a turbo-charger. Knowing we are better together where the whole is greater than the sum of the parts and together we provide for our clients much more holistically than we ever could individually is gratifying. Additionally, it will help our clients as we move forward in introducing them to the network to know there are others out there practicing these economic principles and they do work. What can you learn? Be open to new ideas, seek new wisdom, and be willing to learn from all sources and individuals—even those that you may have taught in the past.

Garrett B. Gunderson and the 3 original partners of Engenuity, Les McGuire, Mike Isom and Ray Hooper were all taught software use by Todd Langford and John Baker and taught The Strategic Coach® concepts by me. When the time came, it wasn't easy for the 3 of us to be willing to be students of the 4 of them. However, setting egos aside and being open-minded and willing to learn enabled us to set aside our teaching hats and become students. Les and Ray's death was a wake up call for all of us and though I'm sorry they are gone, the principles they helped spell out at www.producerpower.com will live in our lives forever. In addition, Garrett Gunderson's creation of the Freedom Fasttrack™ will enable all of us to continue working and growing together.

In order for me to successfully become a part of the Accredited Network, I had to give first. Giving is a major theme I've tried to live in my life for a long time, and when I forget to do it, I fail. When I remember to give first, everyone wins. I recommend that everyone adopt this philosophy. Give first. Create value. It is the way of the wealthy and it can be applied in every area of your life.

My mom, Nancy Lea Hays taught me this concept, but as a teenager I resisted it. She always said as I was heading out "give a good time" instead of "have" a good time. As we often do with things taught to us by our parents, I've now adopted that into my life and I live that principle as often as I can, regretting it when I don't.

Part of my contribution to society is a viable "non-traditional" financial planning firm that enables clients to gain financial confidence, as well as a "visioneering" firm that helps people in all 5 areas of human life value as taught in Freedom Fasttrack™; Financial, Spiritual, Mental, Physical, Social. I attended Principia College where this whole main concept is taught and I'm thrilled to be involved with it again.

Soul Purpose is a constantly expanding and growing concept. I am currently in the process of creating a valuable legacy in the form of a working and self-sufficient alpaca farm in Nacogdoches, Texas, that enables animals and seniors to experience joy together. When it comes to passing on a legacy, I think about my dad, Dan Hays. His gift to me in the fourth grade was a farm to grow up on and a cow to milk. In his own words "we wanted our girls to have chores that would teach them the value of being responsible and how to be responsible by developing a strong work-ethic." I can think of no better legacy to leave to our four children, Jake, Jessica, Robert and Kaylea, than a strong work ethic built around Soul Purpose, which is a sure recipe for creating joy.

# CHAPTER 6

# GREG BLACKBOURN

### Engenuity, Salt Lake City

*Greg Blackbourn is a partner of Engenuity based in Salt Lake City, Utah. As an educator, visionary, and gifted relationship builder, Greg has over decade in the financial services industry as a strategic planner, consultant and coach to successful businesses, families and individuals. By allowing your mind to open up to non-traditional ways of thought you will begin to discover what your true purpose is.*

*Upon graduation from the University of Utah in 1997, Greg entered into the financial services industry. Over the years he learned how institutions focus on product sale and not human life value creation. He discovered that people are assets and products have no intrinsic value. The real value of a product comes with one's abundant mindset.*

*Greg has been continually educating himself though non-traditional forms of education, Mental FastTrack\*, Strategic Coach, LEAP, Landmark Education, multiple financial seminars, as well as multiple books including Killing Sacred Cows, Prosperity Paradigm, Atlas Shrugged, Rich Dad Poor Dad, and many more. On-going Education is the key to a constant self discovery of your Soul Purpose. If you know yourself, you can accomplish anything.*

*Greg married Nicole, his partner in love and in life. They live in Sandy with their four boys (Ryan, Zach, Josh and Drew) and finally baby Ella arriving May 2008. Together they have created a system of education through appreciation of their family. He dedicates a minimum of two hours each week one-on-one with each family member and has not missed a day in a two year time period. He has discovered a unique method to enhance the growth of his family through teaching value principles. His approach has brought great joy and happiness. After all, a families "true wealth" is captured with admiration and since time is a precious asset his dedication provides family growth.*

*Greg's pursuits include ownership in five different businesses, Engenuity Salt Lake City, Prosperity Paradigm, Vitality Life, Rekoneyes Marketing, and a new business teaching family values. He also chairs the Driving for Diabetes golf challenge yearly. The proceeds allow many families to attend a local camp based upon educational values for children with Diabetes.*

*You can contact Greg through his website: http://www.gregblackbourn.com or through email at: gblackbourn@theaccreditednetwork.com, or at: 800-400-5206*

## OVERCOMING ADVERSITY THROUGH SOUL PURPOSE

Ripened experiences of life are the result of engaging a Soul Purpose. One day I arrived at work with a migraine. The pressure clouded my vision and was the pain was unbearable. The migraine was not about to stop me from creating value that day. Instead of clearing the calendar and taking the day off, I cleared my mind, and walked into my first meeting. I repeated to myself, "I am here to create value." No migraine was stopping me from living my Soul Purpose.

Within minutes from the start of the meeting, my migraine went away. My passion of building life-long relationships and empowering others to achieve their highest potential allowed me to block my migraine. My Soul Purpose path was clear, and the migraine didn't stand a chance against my clarity of mind. After the meeting, I knew that I was in my Soul Purpose during the meeting.

When the focus was taken away and the meeting was over, the migraine returned. The next meeting then began and again the migraine subsided. There is a trend to my phenomenon, and it was living in my Soul Purpose. When I was teaching people, and focused on creating tremendous value, I was able to conquer the migraine.

## MY SOUL PURPOSE

I define my Soul Purpose simply: To utilize my ability in developing relationships to help others achieve their highest potential. This has allowed me to become a partner in Engenuity Salt Lake, my primary business. This leadership role allows me to touch the lives of many fantastic people. The relationships I have with associates create some of the most powerful moments of synergy possible. The success of Engenuity Salt Lake is a testament to the effectiveness of Soul Purpose Teams.

Engenuity Salt Lake has transformed the lives of many people by educating them to maximize their human life value. The process helps people to achieve financial freedom as a stepping-stone to their ideal life, giving them permission to dream again, and do what they love in order to be wealthy, healthy, and happy. Myself and the other advisors work to educate the world on the identification and growth of their own Soul Purpose and Soul Purpose Teams that support their endeavors.

## FINDING MY PATH

I was born in Huntington Beach, California. My parents and two older siblings moved to Park City, Utah when I was only three. I recall my childhood and adolescence with fondness, knowing that my parents always gave to me everything they could. My parents taught me everything they believed would help me lead a happy, productive life.

Like most parents from the baby boom generation, they taught me that creating wealth, and pursuing money in a corporate profession was the way to achieve financial independence. This view worked for the post world war generations where there was fear and poverty, yet it did not inspire my personal passion. These lessons from my parents molded my viewpoints throughout my early years and high school.

These lessons taken from my parents created the energy for many Advanced Placement (AP) courses at Park City High school. While there is nothing inherently wrong with taking AP classes, looking back, I see that the AP education actually diluted the power of my education by cramming so many prestigious courses into my schedule. I wonder if my time would have been better utilized to identify other areas in which I felt genuine interest, and focused my attention primarily on those studies. Instead, I received an education in a wide variety of subjects with which I never felt any personal connection.

I briefly contemplated attending either the U.S. Air Force Academy, or the Naval Academy, and pursuing a career as a pilot before college. I realized pilots made good money. Again, I was following money instead of a passion. While feeling no strong calling to the profession, I wisely decided to attend a traditional college.

Enrolled at the University of Utah and still having no real passion, I searched for a major and merely selected one to appease the university registrar. After researching professions Physical Therapy appeared to have a lucrative career. I decided for Pre-Med, and took a series of courses focused on Physical Therapy. I quickly learned that I was not passionate about workings of the human body, and quickly found myself without a major.

Meanwhile at my day job at the Nike Factory Outlet in Park City, I enjoyed the pride of working with customers. A Senior Vice-President from Nike's corporate office came to visit. I worked with him not knowing that he was from the corporate office. The passion I had for serving others shone through, and I somehow impressed the VP, who offered me a job at the Nike's corporate offices in Oregon.  There was only one stipulation; I would have to get a degree in business. With respect for the stature of this man of influence, I took his direction and discovered a love for finance, economics and business in general. The energy and commitment to this new love propelled me to graduate from the University of Utah with a degree in Business Management with a focus on marketing.

However, even though the serendipitous meeting with the Nike VP helped launch me further towards my Soul Purpose, I decided upon graduation that I would stay close to my fiends in Utah. I turned down my guaranteed position at Nike. I understood that I was declining a fabulous opportunity, but the relationships with the people that I had grown to love were stronger than my desire for money.

## BEGINNING A NEW LIFE

I started to search for a position as a stockbroker. The (now old) belief of desire for a money-driven, fast-paced, finance-heavy career of a stockbroker interested me. If schooling taught me anything it was to prepare for the new adventure. I believed my education had built the skills necessary to become a successful stockbroker. Since guidance was lacking, I was easily influenced by my centers of influence at the time. I asked my friends around me for advice. The conclusion was a stockbroker career was not a good fit with my personality. After all a stock broker spends 95% of their time on the phone pitching and accepting trades, and that was not the way to build relationships that I wanted. My friend's recommended I looked at the financial services industry instead where I would have more personal contact with clients.

I wasn't sure which positions were available in the financial services industry that matched my particular ability, so I set up many interviews with insurance/financial companies and searched for the ideal position. At last I found Guardian, one of the largest mutual life insurance companies in the nation. Guardian brought me on board. Here I was, 22 years old and a new life was beginning that would further refine my natural abilities. While working with people one-on-one I found a new joy in assisting people reach their highest financial potential.

Even though working with people gave me great joy, the first several years at Guardian were difficult, to say the least. I was encouraged to sell the companies' products to friends and family to establish a foothold on the industry. My associates assured me that the friends and family's sales was the fastest way to success. The timing for this strategy was not ideal, since most of my friends were either still in school or just surviving in the job market. Unable to sell the big policies, I made a mere $20,000 my first year and begrudgingly accepted financial help from my parents to make ends meet. Near the end of the second year, I looked back only to realize it was a mirror of the first year's struggle. I was dismayed and unsure if I could continue in the financial services industry. Not knowing where to find my next clients was a major concern. But there was light at the end of this second year. I developed a relationship with a person with inner strength and understanding. That relationship would change my life forever. I met Garrett Gunderson.

## NO SUCH THING AS COINCIDENCE

I firmly believe there are no coincidences in life. Garrett was a student at Southern Utah University; and would become an established employee at Guardian. Around this time I also began a family with Nicole, my loving wife. With Garrett's network of influence my life was about to make a drastic change for the better.

Garrett graduated shortly after meeting for the first time, and little did I know my prospects would begin to brighten. We could easily relate to one another's life, lifestyle, and struggles. Our friendship was a natural connection. Garrett began selling large policies to high net-worth clients, and became Guardian's number one producer. Watching with dismay and happiness for me, I sought the ability to replicate Garrett's success. Yet I was lacking in the people aspect in business, and pushed products instead. But I wanted to be a survivor and held on. I redoubled my efforts and had a determination to learn everything I could from Garrett. Shadowing Garrett and bringing him to my own meetings was the beginning of my training. Garrett taught me that the people are the asset. My eyes opened and at that point everything began to change. Garrett was continually attending training seminars around the country, spending thousands of dollars annually to enhance his knowledge and skills, and I began following his example.

Garrett was exceedingly generous with his time and expertise, sharing with me the principles, techniques, and technologies he was using to improve his own practice and grow income. But initially, this new teacher/student relationship between us created a level of dependency. I lacked the self-confidence to close sales on my own. I believed that my own growing success was really just a result only of Garrett's handholding. With the fear of the dependency now realized, what was next? What if I would soon falter and return to my unsuccessful, impoverished past if the relationship changed?

Two things occurred to move me off of the path of dependency and self-consciousness and got me walking on my own. First, I met Steve D'Annunzio and second I met Les McGuire—both relationships developed through Garrett. The transformations that took place with these two people strengthened a whole set of newfound skills.

Garrett had been working with Steve D'Annunzio as a spiritual coach, and recommended that I attend a seminar Steve was presenting. After enrolling at the seminar I learned that my focus was on the wrong principles, with the sales calls. My approach was a data gathering approach, where I entered the call with all the answers and wanted to teach my clients about finances and insurance. However, the truth is that real wealth and success come from seeing people—not products—as the real assets. Why didn't I learn about their dreams and ambitions, and design financial blueprints around the achievement of those desires? Instead of selling insurance products, I learned I should be focused on creating value and seeking relationships. When the value transition occurred, the insurance products would sell themselves as a component of achieving the client's ideal life, Steve taught me. Steve is now my mentor and business partner.

Another major influence was Les McGuire. We formed an immediate friendship. Like Garrett, Les became a mentor to me. While teaching me about the natural principles of wealth creation and sharing his knowledge of the insurance industry, he realized the value of our relationship. Unlike Garrett, however, Les was unwilling to indulge my dependency. Instead, Les even encouraged Garrett to stop doing joint work with me! He correctly believed that it was enabling my self-consciousness, and limiting my personal growth. While Garrett had taught me so many valuable lessons and increased my prosperity. Les understood that the best journeys begin alone with courage to embrace life and conquer without fear.

Les McGuire passed away in a plane crash in June of 2006. For me, Les' death was a tragic wake-up call. I realized that, in his short years on Earth, Les had established a permanent legacy of knowledge and commitment to principles. His legacy lives on in the lives of the people he loved and taught. I then become committed to creating a legacy in my own life's work too.

## THE POWER OF FAMILY

My family has always been the core of my love and relationships. My connection with my wife Nicole was first seeded with love and understanding and has been continually growing ever since. My first child Ryan has taught me valuable lessons has he has overcome great adversity with diabetes. My second child, Zachy is a fun-loving stellar young man. Next is Josh, a wonderful child who is still learning the basics of life. Last is Drew, the youngest and most energetic. I didn't understand the depths that love could reach until I began my own family. The growth of my family has been propelled by my commitment to dedicate time to my family. Time is scheduled to allow for maximum relationship building on a one-to-one basis with every member of my family.

My transformation, largely under Garrett's influence, was the beginning of a great life. I now realize that all of my previous perceptions of life were reevaluated when I met Garrett. I thank him for bringing Steve and Les into my life as well. While my career is important, the key point to success starts in the home with yourself, then your family.

## A TIME OF CHANGE

The spark of Les McGuire's tragic passing started a new path for Greg. Engenuity was established in 2002 with four partners, and now had two. During the daunting task of piecing Engenuity back together after the loss of two amazing founders, I took over Garrett's clients meetings when he moved to Provo.

I phased out Guardian and began a new career at Engenuity, implementing the Innovative Estate Engineering process. I took over all of Garrett Gunderson's client meetings for a six-month period. After the death of Les McGuire and Ray Hooper (both business partners with Garrett) Garrett was challenged with maintaining the operations of the entire business, which were tasks formerly distributed between four partners. Garrett entrusted me to manage my financial advising practice while he implemented systems to build the business of Engenuity.

## NEW DISCOVERIES

Over the next six months, I scheduled thirty client appointments per week. On top of this, I maintained my intense education regimen, which had me traveling cross-country for several days a month. I recall that this period of my life was perhaps the most energizing I have ever experienced. Rather than wearing me out, I felt more alive than ever, because I was truly starting to live my Soul Purpose.

I now knew the value of investing in myself, and enrolled in programs regardless of cost. I attended Landmark Education, Strategic Coach, Mental Fast Track, LEAP (Lifetime Economical Accelerating Process) and many others. I formed relationships with personal and professional coaches. While participating in mentoring conference calls, I began a new journey of self-discovery. I did anything and everything that would foster my own personal growth in the principles of wealth creation. This intense schedule of education and Engenuity brought on tremendous amounts of responsibility. Les' lesson of courage was now manifested in my life.

Being independent, with no more suppression of my power, I was able to accomplish everything I needed to. Garrett, Les and Steve's desire to have me produce without help was validated when I learned two lessons. First, I was quite capable of providing great value to my clients. Second, I was the most important person in my own life.

My lessons are directly applied to my Soul Purpose. This is the fundamental cornerstone of the principled practice of Soul Purpose. People who do not believe they are the most important person in their own life do not take care of themselves adequately. They sacrifice their own wellbeing for others, and inevitably suffer the loss in small or large ways. Taking care of yourself as the most important person in your life creates maximum value for others. Recognizing the importance of self is what gives our Soul Purpose potential. Action of doing what you love gives Soul Purpose power. Without acknowledging self, the ability of one's inborn talents and skills are dismissed, and our capacity to create value for others is unused.

Being the most important person is one's self can be applied to all areas of life. From family, friends to work colleagues and clients—we can maximize value by cherishing ourselves first. I teach the lessons to my four children and wife, that they are the most important person in their own lives. I recognize that establishing this mindset is critical to their ongoing health, wealth, and happiness as working adults in the future. It has nothing to do with selfishness and everything to do with responsibility and creating true, lasting value.

I express my own commitment to self on many levels. Because I treat myself as the most important person in my own life, I view stewardship of my own abilities as a central responsibility. I am constantly working to nurture these abilities, through ongoing training and planning. The seminars, symposiums, books and mentoring add a continual education to "sharpen the saw," as Stephen Covey says. I consider maximizing the protection of my human life value through liability, disability, health, and life insurances as a valuable protection against unforeseen perils, which allows me to have greater peace of mind. Additionally the creations of partnerships, trusts, wills and businesses keep the ones I love most protected. I live by these principles and teach my clients to do the same. Paradoxically, by focusing first on enhancing my own ability to bring value to the marketplace through Soul Purpose, I am able to create more and more value for other people on a daily basis.

## THE POWER OF SOUL PURPOSE

I have experienced first hand the incredible results of committing to one's Soul Purpose. The outcome is staggering, and the changes they bring can even sometimes be humorous. In 2006, I committed to never calculate the commission I would receive from a sale to a client. The reason was the calculation distracted me from my goal of value creation. Several months after developing this habit, I received a call from my wife Nicole. She explained to me that she had found a commission check in their garbage can and asked where it came from. I said, "I don't know, I must have created value for someone." I explained that I had probably absent-mindedly thrown the check away as junk mail. "Absent-mindedly, huh?" Nicole responded. "The check was for $18,000!" I then brought in a system into to assure I would not accidentally throw money away, literally, while still not having to calculate my commissions. However, this experience was an epiphany for me. It allowed me to really feel that money was no longer a reason for helping people. By creating value, the money would follow, but that was no longer my focus.

The virtue of Soul Purpose allows one to stop focusing on money. I had almost tossed out an amount equal to my entire annual earnings several years ago. While I appreciate the money I earn now, I no longer focus on money at all. Truth be told, the reason that I enjoy the wealth I have now is that I am not focused on it. I earn because I create value. In a world of cause and effect, wealth is the cause of value creation, which is nothing but an effect. Soul Purpose means finding what you love, and what you are naturally great at, and using those abilities to create value. I receive great personal meaning and satisfaction in doing what I love. When you live your Soul Purpose in this way, wealth, health, and happiness naturally follow.

My Soul Purpose means cultivating powerful and productive relationships with everyone I know, from my professional colleagues and clients, to my family and friends. I believe that people are stewards only. "We own nothing except our relationships," I like to say. Everything else in our lives are the gifts that God intends us to use to create value in our relationships.

## VALUE CREATION THROUGH SOUL PURPOSE

To create value for my clients, I and the other partners and advisors of Engenuity Salt Lake, use The Freedom FastTrack process developed by Garrett Gunderson and detailed more extensively in other chapters of this book. I value the Freedom FastTrack process, because it is so much more than a marketing pitch for financial products. Through The Freedom FastTrack I can "help people find who they are, and what they love to do." I educate my clients by first understanding them deeply. Instead of a sales pitch, my appointments are unstructured, and begin without a preconceived plan. The education each client receives in the fundamental principles of wealth creation is tailored to that individual client's previous education and understanding. I aim to empower each client by nurturing financial and personal self-reliance. Financial products are implemented only when my clients fully understand them, and choose to move ahead. The due diligence taught on the investments is invaluable. The best part of the system is when their implementation in their comprehensive financial blueprint is executed.

This unique approach to financial education and life coaching has allowed Engenuity Salt Lake to grow astronomically in the past several years. Everyone at Engenuity is taught and trained to focus on creating value for clients. By understanding the principle of value creation, the Engenuity Salt Lake partners, and I know that wealth and prosperity will naturally follow. This commitment has allowed Engenuity to grow into a major, thriving personal coaching company instead of a product-peddling financial services firm.

## SOUL PURPOSE EXPANSION

As I have discovered and expanded my Soul Purpose, I have grown in areas outside of Engenuity Salt Lake, both professionally and personally. I am also a partner or owner of Prosperity Paradigm, LLC, Vitality Life, LLC, and Rekoneyes Marketing, LLC. Each of these companies is another channel through which I can express my Soul Purpose.

Nicole, Ryan, Zach, Josh, and Drew (and daughter Ella on the way) recognize and benefit from my transformation through Soul Purpose as well. My foremost commitment in life is "Alone Time" with each of my family members. No matter what pressing matters demand my attention, I spend at least two hours weekly with each family member. During those two hours, my complete attention is focused on that family member. Ryan now has the confidence to accomplish his dreams. Zach is mastering the art of skateboarding. Josh is adept at understanding value. Drew is learning the importance of love for family. When I spend time with one of my sons, I teach them about the timeless principles of self-reliance, stewardship, Soul Purpose, and value creation. Recently, when my wife Nicole miscarried our fifth child, I found my four-year-old son sweeping the kitchen floor without being asked. When I asked him what he was doing, Josh said "I'm creating value for Mom because she is sick." The results of our Alone Time have strengthened the bonds I feel for my children and beautiful wife more than I ever thought possible.

I am currently writing a book entitled "Alone Time Together (The Enlightened Family): Transforming Your Life Through Structured Commitments to Those You Love Most." It will teach, and hopefully inspire, others to achieve and enjoy the same results I have found through my family's practice of spending quality time together.

# CHAPTER 7

# PHILIP TIRONE
## Seven Steps to 720

*An expert in residential home financing, Philip X. Tirone has a unique background in difficult-to-obtain loans, having started his career working with borrowers with stated income and/or subprime credit scores. With this foundation, he became a specialist in the credit scoring process, authoring the book, 7 Steps To a 720 Credit Score™.*

*Philip is the founder of The Mortgage Equity Group (The MEG) and specializes in educating borrowers and helping them increase their credit scores so they qualify for the optimal loan programs available. The MEG is a non-traditional mortgage company composed primarily of team members committed to providing each homebuyer with specialized time and services unique to his or her needs, complementing traditional mortgage services with innovative programs aimed at reducing mortgage payments and maximizing buying power.*

*Philip's commitment to educating homebuyers prompted him to create the 7 Steps Licensing Program in which he trains other mortgage planners on consistently outperforming the market by helping clients improve their credit scores. As well, he established the 7 Steps Foundation, a charitable fund that allocates resources to help low-income and underserved Americans increase their credit scores.*

*Philip has an uncanny ability to develop innovative strategies to simplify any process. Most recently, he created The Home Loan Maximizer™, a program that allows homeowners to purchase larger homes while maintaining the same monthly payments. His Complete Financial Navigator™ analyzes his borrowers' needs and financial picture, thereby helping borrowers overcome barriers to achieving their real estate goals. As a frequent guest lecturer at the University of California Los Angeles, Philip has authored and delivered numerous speeches about avoiding the "Mortgage Lifestyle Dilemma," a phrase he coined to describe an emotional buying decision that results in overextension and a life that revolves around high mortgage payments.*

*Philip and his programs have been featured in the Los Angeles Times, New York Times.com, Wall Street Journal, Newsday, Woman's World Magazine, San Jose Mercury News, San Francisco Chronicle, Bottom Line Magazine, Bankrate.com, among others. He was recently featured in the New York Times bestseller, Secrets of the Young & Successful. As well, in 2008, he will be featured in Dan Sullivan's new book, Industry Transformers, which identifies eight individuals with are having a profound impact on their industry by creating meaningful ways for their clients to bypass the bureaucracy and the "red tape" which most consumers face.*

*Named Arizona State University's Man of the Year in 1994, Philip currently resides in Los Angeles with his wife, Lily, and daughter, Ava. Philip can be reached at: (877) 720-SCORE (7267) or by visiting www.7StepsTo720.com*

## WHY ARE YOU SO PASSIONATE ABOUT CREDIT?

Your three-digit credit score can have a six-digit impact on your finances, yet credit scoring bureaus refuse to divulge the rules of the credit game. People are turned down for loans, unable to attain the American Dream, and struggle financially because of the closely guarded secrets of credit score. Exposing the rules of this game means that countless Americans can save hundreds, sometimes thousands, of dollars in interest payments. And this savings can change the course of a person's life.

## HOW IS CREDIT IMPORTANT?

Let's put this into perspective: At least four out of every 10 people are paying higher mortgages than they would if they took a few simple steps to increase their credit. And on a $300,000 home loan, the difference between poor credit (under 620) and good credit (720 and above) is $589 a month, or $212,040 over the life of a 30-year loan. According to a 2004 U.S. Public Interest Research Group Survey, almost 80 percent of consumers have errors on their credit reports, and 25 percent have errors serious enough to cause them to be turned down for loans or jobs.

That's right: Some employers won't consider hiring you if your credit score is low. If you have bad credit, you will have problems finding an apartment to rent, much less a home to buy. You will search frantically for a car loan, only to be disheartened by large monthly payments due to sky-high interest rates. Even your automobile insurance premiums will be higher. Savings for your child's college tuition? A nice vacation? Forget about it—you can't afford them if your credit is poor. And if you decide to take a vacation anyway, you will likely charge it to your high-interest credit card, further adding to your financial hardships. This risky spending and subsequent compound interest can quickly spiral downward; you might miss a payment or two. Before you know it, you are being hounded at home and at the office be aggressive collection agencies demanding payment on your delinquent financial accounts. Complicating matters, you have to deal with the embarrassment of creditors calling your home and office all day.

On the other hand, if your credit is good, lenders will compete for your business. You will qualify for the best loans on cars, homes, boats, furniture, or whatever you might choose to buy. Throughout the course of your life, you will save hundreds of dollars in interest, money you can apply to retirement savings, your child's college tuition, or investments. Countless offers for credit cards will food your mailbox, and you will have a padded bank account that allows you to buy vacation homes, start businesses, or retire early. Moreover, you will have peace of mind.

## WHAT ARE THE FACTORS THAT COMPRISE A CREDIT SCORE?

Though your credit score is based on approximately 22 different criteria, five factors make up the bulk of the formula: 1) your payment history comprises 35 percent of your score; 2) the amount of money you owe accounts for 30 percent; 3) the length of time you have had credit is used to consider 15 percent of your score; 4) 10 percent of your score is determined by the type of credit you have; and 5) the remaining 10 percent is determined by the number and frequency of credit inquiries.

## WHAT IS CONSIDERED BAD CREDIT? AND WHAT IS GOOD CREDIT?

If you have a credit score of 720 or above, then you have wonderful credit and will qualify for loans and interest rates for borrowers in the highest echelon.

If you have a credit score of 700 to 719, then you have excellent credit and are considered low risk, but you might not qualify for the best loans and your interest rates might drop if you raised your score a few points.

If you have a credit score of 660 to 699, then you have fair to good credit. You might qualify for a strong loan, but only if the rest of your application is strong. You definitely won't receive the best loans of the lowest interest rates.

If you have a credit score to 620 to 659, then your have weak to borderline credit. The rest of your file will need to be perfect to qualify for an acceptable loan. You will pay higher interest rates and your loan terms will be less than ideal, assuming you even qualify for a loan.

If you have a credit score below 620, you have poor credit. Your loan terms—if you qualify—will be far from ideal. You pay the highest interest rates. The lower your score, the worse your terms, and the less likely you are to qualify at all.

## I WANT TO INCREASE MY CREDIT SCORE. WHERE DO I BEGIN?

Before beginning anything, first let me congratulate you for taking ownership of your financial future. Bravo! The most empowered place to start any journey is with the truth. To that end, request a copy of your credit report from each of the three major bureaus: Equifax, Experian, and TransUnion. Contrary to popular belief, your credit score will not be hurt by requesting your report. (Credit inquiries only hurt your score when they are initiated by potential lenders such as a auto dealership, credit card company, or bank.) Feel free to request your own credit report every six months, or even more as you work to improve the score.

Note that your credit report and credit score are not the same thing. Your report is a list of all your accounts, your payment history related to those accounts, and inquiries (those initiated by you and those initiated by lenders). Your score is the resultant rating derived from the information listed on your credit report. You will be able to find your credit report for free, but your credit score will cost extra (approximately $15). Note that there are three credit bureaus (Experian, TransUnion, and Equifax). Depending on who is requesting your score, the bureaus will apply different formulas to calculate the score. In other words, the score you see might be very different from the score lenders will see. I once pulled my report the same day my mortgage broker pulled my report: The two scores varied by 70 points! Regardless, your credit report will give a ballpark idea of the credit improvement steps you need to take.

## WHAT IS ONE OF THE MOST IMPORTANT THINGS I CAN DO TO IMPROVE MY CREDIT SCORE?

In Step 1 of my book, 7 Steps to a 720 Credit Score, I discuss the importance and impact that your utilization rate has on your score. The utilization rate is the debt you carry on a credit card in proportion to your balance. The balance of any one credit card should never exceed 30 percent of your limit. For instance, if you have a $10,000 limit on your Visa card, keep your total charges at no more than $3,000.

So how do you lower your utilization rate? Paying down the debt is the best remedy, but one that admittedly is not available to most people with credit card debt. After all, if you have a substantial amount of disposable income, you would not likely be carrying credit card debt in the first place. Rest assured, there are craftier and more likely options to lowering the rate, such as: 1) transferring a fraction of funds from one card to another so that each card has a 30 percent balance or less; and/or 2) asking your credit card company to increase your limit so that the balance is less than 30 percent; and/or 3) opening another credit card account and transferring balances accordingly (but only after reading Step Two: Have at Least Three Revolving Credit Lines of my book, 7 Steps to a 720 Credit Score).

## WHAT IS ONE OF THE MOST IMPORTANT THINGS I CAN DO TO IMPROVE MY CREDIT SCORE?

Not unless you can keep the utilization rate less than 30 percent on this card. In an effort to save money, people often transfer numerous credit card balances to a lower (or zero) interest rate card, carrying all debt on this card, which is pushing a 100 percent utilization rate. The truth is that this approach will initially save money if you carry a balance, but at what cost? By carrying one card with a 100 percent utilization rate, your credit score will suffer. Remember the domino affect that a low credit score can have on a person's life? A low credit score can cost you hundreds of thousands of dollars in higher interest rates. In the long run, this strategy could hurt you, especially if you are planning on buying a home or car within the next six months. Instead, remember, the lower your utilization rate, the higher your credit score. Instead, try to keep all credit cards under a 30 percent utilization rate.

## MY AMERICAN EXPRESS CARD HAS NO SPENDING LIMIT, HOW THEN DOES THE CREDIT BUREAU DETERMINE MY UTILIZATION RATE?

On cards with no preset spending limits, credit bureaus report your credit limit using the highest balance you have ever had on your credit card. This throws your utilization rate out of whack if you generally spend the same amount from month to month. To avoid exceeding your target rate, you can try this tactic: Spend one month "hiking up" your balance as high as possible, thereby increasing the high credit limit to a high enough mark that you do not exceed the 30 percent utilization rate in subsequent months.

## WHAT IS THE MOST SHOCKING CREDIT SECRET AROUND?

There are two, and I cannot decide which is sleazier. The first is called the Universal Default Clause. This clause allows a credit card to raise your interest rate if another credit card reports your account as past due. Imagine this: You have four credit cards, all with interest rates below 10 percent. You arrive to work one day and your employer informs you that he is going out of business and you are without a job. You liquidate some assets and scramble to find another job. Unfortunately, you are late on your MasterCard payment. The next month, you notice that your MasterCard, as well as your Visa, Discover, and American Express cards all have a 29.9 percent interest rate.

Credit card companies periodically pull your credit report and raise your interest rate based on the history of other accounts you maintain. This "Universal Default Clause" is a fine print item that credit card companies don't want you to know about. They say that your behavior on one credit card might be the same on all credit cards. I say that it's a way for credit card companies to charge you a high interest rate even if your payment has been perfect on their credit card.

The second shocking credit secret is that credit card companies often intentionally report a lower limit than you actually have. Why do they do this? This makes you less desirable to competing credit card companies how might solicit your business if they knew your true balance. Unfortunately, a lower credit limit can throw your utilization out of whack and artificially lower your score. So when you pull your credit report, check to see that your limit is accurately reported on each account.

## WHAT IS THE BEST WAY TO GET COLLECTION ACCOUNTS OFF MY CREDIT REPORT?

Believe it or not, you will do more harm than good to your credit by paying off an account in collections, especially if the account is over two years old. Bills that have been turned over for collection affect your score only minimally after two years and are all but erased after four years. But each time you make a payment on a bill in collection, you create new activity on the account, which renews: 1) the length of time the account stays on your report; and 2) the currency of the derogatory account. You also hurt your credit score even further. Because inactive items fall off the account in seven years and new items are weighted more heavily than old items, it is often better for your credit score (but not your conscience!) to let sleeping dogs lie.

Because your debts are your responsibility, you should always pay accounts in collection, but be strategic to make sure the payment doesn't renew the activity and hurt your score. If you have a bill that has been in collection, you should not pay it until you negotiate an agreement from the creditor or collection company to submit a letter of deletion to the credit bureau asking that the derogatory item be wiped from your credit report.

If you have items in collection, be sure to read Step 6: Negotiate for a Letter of Deletion Before Paying a Bill that Is in Collection of my book, 7 Steps to a 720 Credit Score.

## IS IT POSSIBLE TO HAVE TOO FEW OR TOO MANY CREDIT CARD ACCOUNTS?

Yes and yes. Less credit does not equal a better score. Credit scores awarded higher scores to people with between three and five revolving accounts. Why this number? Lenders want to be sure that you will not abuse your credit privileges. If you have too few accounts, bureaus don't have proof that you can manage multiple accounts. In fact, no credit is just as bad as poor credit. Credit bureaus want to see that you can handle credit responsibly, and the best way to prove that you can handle accounts responsibly is by having a healthy mix of credit and a solid payment history.

On the other hand, if you have too many accounts, bureaus might think you have overextended yourself. However, do not close accounts. Pay down the balance and keep the cards open and active. Credit experts generally agree that closing accounts might hurt you score by lowering your overall utilization rate and shortening the average age of your active accounts. Keeping accounts active protects you from suffering lowered limits, a byproduct of inactive accounts.

## HOW CAN I PROTECT MY CREDIT DURING MY DIVORCE?

If you are going through a divorce, immediately refinance your home and cancel any joint credit card accounts. If your spouse retains ownership of the home without refinancing, your credit will be damaged if your spouse becomes delinquent on payments. Some people mistakenly believe that the divorce decree and quitclaim deed with rescue them from any repercussions if a former spouse becomes delinquent on his house payment. Unfortunately, the agreement you had with your bank remains in effect until your former spouse refinances under his name. And what if you keep the home without refinancing in your name solely? In some states, a lawsuit filed against your spouse can result in your home being taken as part of the settlement.

For the same reason, cancel all jointly held credit cards.

## SHOULD MARRIED COUPLES AVOID JOINT CREDIT ALL TOGETHER?

Couples are best served by establishing credit separately. In fact, it puts them at an advantage in the credit game as they can leverage each other's credit when necessary. For instance, if you need a new line of credit you can transfer a portion of your balance to your spouse's card, thereby lowering your utilization rate and qualifying for the best interest rate available. Also, individual lines of credit protect both parties from losing complete ownership of their credit score.

## SHOULD MARRIED COUPLES AVOID JOINT CREDIT ALL TOGETHER?

Couples are best served by establishing credit separately. In fact, it puts them at an advantage in the credit game as they can leverage each other's credit when necessary. For instance, if you need a new line of credit you can transfer a portion of your balance to your spouse's card, thereby lowering your utilization rate and qualifying for the best interest rate available. Also, individual lines of credit protect both parties from losing complete ownership of their credit score.

## ARE THERE ANY TYPES OF CREDIT THAT WILL HURT MY SCORE?

Generally speaking, installment loans are key to establishing a healthy mix of credit and securing the best credit score, but one kind of installment loan will always hurt your score.

But let's start first with helpful installment loans. An installment loan is a purchase agreement whereby the borrower repays the loan in equal periodic payments and the loan is secured through a piece of property. Cars, boats, furniture, and computers are typical items bought through installment loans. A car lease is another type of installment loan. If you do not have an installment loan, or if you have an installment loan that is detrimental to your score (for instance, if you had too many late payments or a car that was repossessed), you should add an installment loan to your credit report.

But be wary of any installment loan that delays payment for more than 30 days. If you purchase a television in June and are told that you do not need to make payments until February, you are hurting your score with a harmful installment account. These types of accounts are most often offered in furniture, electronic, or appliance stores, and they can be tricky to spot. If you are offered a "buy now, pay in 18 months" credit account, you are likely being offered a harmful installment loan, which suggests that you are in a financial bind and cannot afford to make immediate payments, a situation credit bureaus see as risky. Never apply for these types of loans unless you can afford to see your credit score drop.

## ARE THERE ANY TYPES OF CREDIT THAT WILL HURT MY SCORE?

Generally speaking, installment loans are key to establishing a healthy mix of credit and securing the best credit score, but one kind of installment loan will always hurt your score.

But let's start first with helpful installment loans. An installment loan is a purchase agreement whereby the borrower repays the loan in equal periodic payments and the loan is secured through a piece of property. Cars, boats, furniture, and computers are typical items bought through installment loans. A car lease is another type of installment loan. If you do not have an installment loan, or if you have an installment loan that is detrimental to your score (for instance, if you had too many late payments or a car that was repossessed), you should add an installment loan to your credit report.

But be wary of any installment loan that delays payment for more than 30 days. If you purchase a television in June and are told that you do not need to make payments until February, you are hurting your score with a harmful installment account. These types of accounts are most often offered in furniture, electronic, or appliance stores, and they can be tricky to spot. If you are offered a "buy now, pay in 18 months" credit account, you are likely being offered a harmful installment loan, which suggests that you are in a financial bind and cannot afford to make immediate payments, a situation credit bureaus see as risky. Never apply for these types of loans unless you can afford to see your credit score drop.

## IF I'M BUYING A HOME, WHAT SHOULD I KNOW ABOUT CREDIT?

When applying for a home loan, nothing is more important than your credit score. In fact, your credit score accounts for about 70 percent of your loan application. However, it isn't the only factor. Lenders will determine your credit-worthiness by looking at your credit, your income, your savings (both before and after closing the loan), and your down payment. But if you have a 720 credit score, some lenders might not consider your savings or your income at all! Remember, 720 is the magic number that will bring you one step closer to the American Dream: owning a home. Your credit score not only determines whether you will overpay on home loan, but it also determines whether you will qualify for a home loan at all.

If you are improving your credit so that you can buy a home, start the credit improvement process early. Ideally, you would start at least 24 months in advance if your score falls below a 620 and a year in advance if your score is lower than a 720.

Your first step should be to find a lender and ask him to pull your credit report. If your score is less than 720, ask your lender what this score tells him about your borrowing ability. If your lender doesn't suggest that you work to increase your credit score to 720, you have the wrong lender. Call (877) 720-SCORE for a referral to a lender who will help you maximize your score and minimize your interest payments.

## I'M A MORTGAGE PLANNER WHOSE CLIENTS WOULD BENEFIT FROM CREDIT IMPROVEMENT. WHERE CAN I GET MORE INFORMATION THAT WOULD HELP ME BUILD MY BUSINESS?

With the bottom dropping out of the mortgage industry, it seems that all mortgage brokers are standing atop a slippery slope. This question is no longer: What loan can I get for my client? Instead, the question is: Can I get a loan for my client? Will we find a loan before another credit crunch causes the guidelines to change again, making thousands of homeowners ineligible for mortgages?

To help mortgage brokers differentiate themselves during a changing real estate environment, we have created the 7 Steps Licensing Program. This program allows mortgage professionals to continue growing their business by helping clients improve their credit scores and qualify for even the strictest of loans. To differentiate yourself and keep your practice powered during a downturn in the market, contact us today at 877-720-SCORE.

**With this licensing program, you will learn:**

1. *Shocking credit secrets that hurt your clients' scores and lower their likelihood of qualifying for a loan.*

2. *The dirty little trick credit card companies use to lower your clients' credit scores.*

3. *How a client can rebuild credit after a foreclosure or bankruptcy.*

4. *The type of credit that will always hurt and never help a score.*

5. *The fastest ways to improve your clients' credit scores so that they can qualify for the best loan.*

6. *Marketing ideas for applying the 7 Steps to increase your mortgage volume, even when the market is down.*

7. *How to set themselves apart from other lending professionals by exploiting their position as a licensed 7 Steps lender.*

8. *How subprime borrowers can quickly become desired borrowers by applying the7 Steps.*

## I'M AN ADVISOR (FINANCIAL ADVISOR, REAL ESTATE AGENT, INSURANCE AGENTS, ACCOUNTANT, OR OTHERWISE) INTERESTED IN BUILDING MY BOOK OF BUSINESS AND AT THE SAME TIME DIFFERENTIATING MYSELF FROM THE COMPETITION. HOW WOULD I DO THAT?

The 7 Steps Licenicng Program is also available to advisors in the real estate or financial industries. This program allows you to build your business by leveraging your position as a credit expert. Licensed professionals learn detailed information about the credit scoring process as well as marketing strategies such as "Lunch and Learns," whereby they present the 7 Steps to clients and/or employees.

For more information, call us at 877-720-SCORE (7267).

## WHAT IF I NEED MORE HELP RAISING MY CREDIT SCORE?

In today's environment, credit is more important than ever. Unless your credit is flawless, many banks won't lend to a borrower, much less provide strong terms or refinance existing loans. If your credit is less-than-perfect, start improving it today by calling 877-720-SCORE (7267) or by visiting www.7Stepsto720.com, where you will find information about the 7 Steps to a 720 Credit Score book and workbook. Also, look at our 7 Steps Credit Intensive program whereby one of our 7 Steps representative will analyze your credit report and personally coach you as to what you need to do to raise your credit score to 720 or above. Remember, with a 720 credit score, banks will compete for your business and you will get the best loan available!

# CHAPTER 8

# DEE RANDALL
## Horizon Financial

Dee A. Randall is a committed entrepreneur in the Insurance and other financial services industry. He began his working career in the retail and manufacturing industry. Dee began his career in the financial arena in September 1986. Starting in the life insurance industry he developed very early a passion for permanent life insurance.

Dee practices the "Wealth In Motion" strategies that the Horizon Financial Advisors teach their clients. Together with his family they strive to live the Abundant Life principles taught in The Abundant Life Model for the Community. Dee carries the maximum amount of Permanent Life Insurance coverage that the insurance companies will allow as he strives to protect his Human Life Value. He strives to live daily his Soul Purpose governed by his religious beliefs.

Dee is the Founder and President of Horizon Financial and Insurance Group, The Abundant Life Model for the Community, The Abundant Life Model for Advisors, Independent Financial and Investments, Horizon Auto Funding, and Maple Apartments.

To contact Dee for information about his companies or for other personal or career questions call 800-400-5206 or email him at dee@horizonfinancial.com.

Websites are www.horizonfinancial.com and www.theabundantlifeexperience.com

## DEFINING SOUL PURPOSE

I define Soul Purpose as my Unique Ability is "to work creatively and strategically with people, supporting them without reservation as they try to reach their highest potential. I know that when I invest time and resources, unselfishly in helping others achieve their dreams, I will also reach my dreams." Specifically, I thrive on helping people build legacies.

The life insurance planning service provides significant opportunity to be involved in the lives of both clients and advisors and help them in their efforts to reach their dreams. I am the president and founder of Horizon Financial, a group of over 100 advisors throughout the United States. Each advisor is committed to assist their clients with the finest financial education and support possible. I also own Independent Financial, a securities Investment firm offering strong support with other financial products; and am the founder of The Abundant Life Model for The Community, whose soul purpose is to assist clients in building legacies to last for generations.

## DISCOVERING SOUL PURPOSE

It was only in 2006 that I articulated my Unique Ability or Soul Purpose into words that could be expressed in a clear, manageable way. However, I began to discover my Soul Purpose long before I knew what it was, when I was serving a mission for The Church of Jesus Christ of Latter-day Saints in 1970. It became clearer to me a few years later in 1973. This is the time when my wife Patricia and I were visiting my mother-in-Law in Eastern Canada shortly after we were married.

My mother-in-Law gave me some cassette tapes of Earl Nightengale.On reflection I am sure she gave me the tapes to help motivate me to make something of myself so I could take care of her daughter. A few months later, I was listening to the tapes and heard him say "you can get anything you desire in life if you will help others get what they want."

Those words struck me that day, and they have moved me from that day to this. If you misuse them in a self-serving or manipulative way, it does not serve you or the ones you are trying to help. You will have short-term results but not long lasting, or what I would call "abundant relationship", but you can understand why these words were the foundation of what I would now call my Unique Ability or Soul Purpose.

These words are what give my life "Human Life Value", and what allows me to increase the "Human Life Value" of those I associate with.

## LIVING SOUL PURPOSE

It is certainly true with me, as I'm sure it is with most people, that there are times when it is a challenge to always be functioning in your Soul Purpose. I find that, day in and day out, as I assume the responsibilities I have in my businesses, it can become difficult to stay focused. What personally helps me the most, is working with qualified, talented team members who are also striving to work in their specific abilities. It is a privilege to be around such strong, independent, and talented financial advisors who serve their clients so well. These are the very individuals with whom it is my privilege to work with. I get great satisfaction from helping them achieve their dreams, as they strive to help their clients reach theirs.

I have found that if you really have found your Soul Purpose or Unique Ability, and it is in reality "who you are", it is natural for you to act. If you have contrived it so it will sound good to others then you will constantly struggle with it. In other words, Soul Purpose doesn't bring real success when it isn't genuine and sincere.

When I am living in my Soul Purpose, I experience the greatest satisfaction. Looking back over the years I would say that to any extent that I have had a life of abundance, it has been when I have been able to help others. More specifically, helping and watching advisors build their own independent practice, while assisting their clients in building their future has brought lasting satisfaction.

I have many more great years ahead of me, and a lifetime of great years behind me. For that reason it is nearly impossible to identify a single moment when I figured it all out. There are so many from the past, and there will certainly be many more in the future. But in the context of my Soul Purpose, my "Ah Ha" moments have come from watching my grown children excel in something that they—in some small way—learned from me. That is the most satisfying use of my Soul Purpose.

When I have to make difficult decisions, or when I am in difficult circumstances, I rely on three fundamental sources. First, I review or reflect on fundamental principles and truths that I know to be true. Second, I try to seek the advice of those around me whose judgment and experience I have found to be sound. Third, I rely always on faith and prayer for answers and constant guidance.

Too often in life we give all the glory to the one that finishes "number one" or whose Soul Purpose by its very nature is out front on stage. Not everyone seems to get equal recognition for their excellence, but what really inspires me is anyone in any work, who excels in their occupation or in the arena of their own stewardship, such as the waitress who graciously serves me while I'm eating out, the craftsman who comes to my home and is able to fix what I can't, the teacher who inspires my children to learn, the doctor who cares for my injuries, and the tour guide who knows his or her subject well, just as a few examples. These are the ones that make all our lives better and inspire me to do better at what I have chosen to do.

## CHOOSING A PATH

People ask me why I do what I do. For one thing, we live in a day and time in history where money plays such a big role in our lives. Money supports our efforts to create Human Life Value for our selves and for those around us. It is therefore important to understand how it works, how to make it work for us, how to protect it, and how to use it in building a legacy for our generation and future generations.

I do what I do because those advisors who are part of Horizon are striving to help their clients create those legacies, and I want to be a part of that effort. I also do what I do with our "Abundant Life Model" because it helps families understand their True Assets and to transfer those True Assets to future generation, while enjoying them now. What I like best is helping people, and helping advisors and clients create Human Life Value beyond their expectations.

I chose this path because it's something I'm good at, and something I enjoy. I have been in this specific profession for 21 years, with over 38 years of business and management experience. Specifically I have the financial and management background to build a producer group of like minded individuals committed to supporting their clients, and a lifetime of experience learning to understand (in some small way at least) the desire people have to pass their legacy to those around them and to their future generations.

## OUR MISSION

Our process or model is the "Abundant Life Model for Advisor"s, and the "Abundant Life Model for the Community". Our mission at Horizon Financial is simply to be the leading agency/producer group in the country in helping advisors and their clients reach their real Human Life Potential through these models.

Clients get involved with our process by working with one of the advisors associated with Horizon and our Abundant Life Models. Either as an advisor, or as a client, you will learn the value of creating and enjoying legacies now, and in the future. We can live lives of abundance if we strive to make masterpieces of our lives, and our models help individuals know how to do so. I strive to help as many people as possible reach their greatest potential. In a nutshell, I everyone I work with, whether an advisor or a client, to live every area of their lives more abundantly because we crossed paths.

*To contact Dee for information about his companies, or for other personal or career questions, call 800-400-5206 or email him at dee@horizonfinancial.com.

Websites are www.horizonfinancial.com and www.theabundantlifeexperience.com

# PHIL MANNING
## Manning Investment Group

Philip Manning received his MBA degree in the fields of international Management and his B.S. degree in Business Management and Education. For over twenty-two years he has worked in various areas of the financial industry.

Mr. Manning began as a financial analyst for RCA Corp. After leaving RCA, he helped build a small, start-up investment advisory firm with assets of $9 million, to a respected firm that managed over $250 million, in less than three years. He was one of the largest institutional clients of Merrill Lynch on the west coast and was a client of other well-known firms such as Goldman Sachs, Solomon Brothers, Smith Barney etc. Eventually, Mr. Manning worked for some of those large brokerage firms.

Later in his career, he was hired as a consultant for a publicly traded company. Eventually he was hired full time by the firm and he became a Vice President with the role of assisting that company in raising millions of dollars and increasing the value of the company's stock through sound management.

For several years Philip served in management for one of the largest proprietary trading firms in America. Later, Mr. Manning was hired as the head of trading for a European investment bank, but had to resign for health reasons. Since that time, He has been self-employed as a financial consultant, a professional equities trader and business owner. His breadth of experience has given him the opportunity to develop a unique and *profound understanding of investment and finance. Mr. Manning has managed investments for corporations high-net-worth individuals. He brings an expansive and highly-qualified view of finance and investment to the service of his clients.*

*Because of his background, Mr. Manning is able to introduce to clients, financial concepts and practices which are not widely known or practiced and therefore not generally available to most investors. Philip teaches clients the truth about investments and finance. He dispels myths about investing that keep most investors mired in mediocrity. He has an innate ability to teach clients innovative principles of wealth creation and management in a way that makes complex subjects understandable, which imbues his clients with the knowledge and confidence necessary to know the are making the best possible decisions regarding the financial aspects of their lives.*

## SOUL PURPOSE

Anyone who works with a member of the Accredited Network or who has had any connection with the Freedom Fast Track process is aware of the term "Soul purpose". My soul purpose is teaching people. I discovered my soul purpose while teaching foreign language, business and time management classes to young college-aged students. In the context of my career, teaching involves transferring my knowledge of the investment world to clients, in a way that they can understand and that allows them to develop a belief that the decisions they are taking at my recommendation, are truly in their best interest. I believe complex financial principles can be presented in a way that they are easy to understand. I take great satisfaction in working with clients who become 100% committed to what we are accomplishing together, because I have helped them gain sufficient knowledge, to be confident in the wealth strategies they are implementing. For me, there is no greater moment than watching someone's countenance change completely when "a light goes on" and I know they have understood what I have taught them.

## LIVING SOUL PURPOSE

Living my soul purpose brings professional satisfaction to me and is beneficial for my clients. Most of the time, living my soul purpose is easy. However, at times living my soul purpose is made more difficult because of incorrect business paradigms that exist. In the finance and investment world, too much focus is placed on "closing the deal", "making the sale" or generally making things happen quickly. I have never been a believer in "power selling" or employing sales "tactics". In my experience people want to understand what they are accepting or rejecting and resent "hard sell" tactics. The understanding what clients desire, can usually occur only if teaching and learning are taking place. A true teacher will strive to clarify, while a salesman thrives on knowing more than the client and benefits from keeping the client a little confused.

Throughout my career, I have had so many people thank me for teaching them the truth instead of forcing something upon them. In those cases I usually didn't make a "sale" but the good will created, proved to be far more valuable. After someone compliments me for being honest or for telling them the way things really work, even though we weren't able to do business, it is very easy and natural to accept the compliment by responding with a request that they refer friends or family who would appreciate a similar, honest and ethical approach. The vast majority of my new client relationships have come through referrals. Many times the referrals came from someone I didn't do business with. To avoid the conflicts between the world's view of getting business done or "selling" and my belief in and love of teaching, I have been self-employed most of my career. I insist on doing business with clients in an atmosphere where teaching and learning are taking place.

## TEACHING OUTSIDE OF THE CLASSROOM

Following my soul purpose of teaching has allowed me to create meaningful, life-long relationships with clients and associates. Not being hobbled by the belief that teaching only takes place in a classroom, has allowed me to foster a rewarding career in finance and investment. While I have great respect for the teachers in our nation's schools, I know many who feel crippled by the bureaucratic and institutional demands to teach in a certain way for a particular outcome. Many teachers today feel like all creativity has been stripped away by government intervention. But what so many teachers fail to realize is that teachers are needed everywhere in society and not just in the classroom. I have been blessed to be able to combine my love of teaching and my excitement about investment. Most people think of me as a money manager, investment adviser or financial expert. In my mind, I am a teacher.

## AN "AHA" MOMENT

I have been asked what one of my greatest "Aha" moments is and when it occurred. This moment relates to another faulty business paradigm that sometimes makes living my soul purpose difficult. For me it happened as I was contemplating the question of a client, regarding the cost and complexity of a financial product being sold by one of the large Wall Street firms I worked for. Early in my career it dawned on me that every product sold by a Wall Street brokerage firm, a bank or insurance company, is created to make the company money. Sure, every product is purported to fill some need, but always, in every case, the benefit to the company is considered before the benefit to the client. Following right on the heels of that "Aha" moment was another related discovery. It was, that most of the financial products pawned off on unsuspecting investors, wouldn't even exist if our own government wasn't complicit in passing the very laws that created the "need" for these products. Politicians' most powerful motivation is power. They have a need to be re-elected to retain that power. To do so, they play a corrupt game with highly paid lobbyists. Like all other sectors of the economy, the investment firms have their lobbyists. Many are attorneys, and it is these people who suggest and even help write the very laws our congress passes. It is these laws that make these financial products "necessary". It was a sobering reality. Because of the craving for power, politicians will hurt the very citizens they are supposed to protect. In the majority of cases, investors would be better off without the new laws and the accompanying new financial products. Investors have paid a terrible price for these "unholy alliances". A study of the crash of 2000 reveals that it was these very alliances at work that caused the crash and the billions of dollars of losses by small investors. Since that realization, I have spent my career, teaching clients about the "true" road to financial freedom. It is not an easy task because investors have been told over and over how they should save and invest. The problem is, investors are unwittingly playing into the hands of politicians and their corrupt partners in industry. Breaking these paradigms and getting clients to believe that the true road to financial freedom requires them to do the opposite of what the government and institutions tell them is often difficult. It requires investors to take action based on new learning and new paradigms. It takes courage to implement the new concepts they have learned. That is precisely why investors must be carefully taught and not simply "sold to".

## LIVING BY PRINCIPLE

Once I realized that the vast majority of investment businesses are driven by motives like those I described above, I was determined that I would only be involved in the financial world if I could live and work by the principles I believed in. Since the time of those realizations, I have tried to base all of my decisions on principle; from the employers I work for, to the clients I represent, to the products I work with, I try to "put my money" where my principles are.

This can be challenging. Early in my career, I decided to leave a very lucrative and promising position with a "great" firm, because I simply could not work and live by their business principles. At the time, the decision was excruciatingly difficult, because I knew I was walking away from a small fortune. But once the decision was made and I was gone, I never looked back… well, maybe just a couple of times, so I could be reminded of exactly how expensive my principles were. Making difficult decisions can be hard if we are always looking through a financial lens. But when we look through the lens of our principles, most decisions are clear and not that difficult to make.

In the investment world, living and working by principle can get lonely and difficult. When I struggle and wonder why the unprincipled and unethical seem to get ahead or when I watch people making decisions that impact my life, based on greed or even some lesser principle; I always have one place I turn for inspiration, my wife. She, like many dedicated spouses, is my number one supporter. She never doubts and never second-guesses my principles. In addition to being a great source of comfort and inspiration, my wife is a phenomenal source of great business ideas. When I was younger and more foolish, I would come home anxious about some perplexing business problem. She would often listen and then give advice. I would dismiss her advice with a lecture that went something like: "This deal is complicated and it's just not as simple as you think." Over the years I began to notice a pattern. The things my wife predicted often came true. Her advice seemed to be right "on the money". Even though she did not have an advanced business degree, she was intuitive and intelligent. In time I learned to turn to her not only for inspiration but also for sound, excellent business advice. I believe that to achieve true financial freedom, couples have to develop a relationship based on mutual respect and interest in the ideas and concerns of one another.

## TEACHING TRUE PRINCIPLES TO OTHERS

Another reason that my wife inspires me is that she understands the reasons that I do the work I do. She understands my passion for teaching and that as a teacher my first priority is not making a sale. The reason I manage investments for clients is that I believe I have unique knowledge and experience that can protect them from the unethical practices of the investment community and provide them with powerful solutions they will not find anywhere else. If I teach clients true principles of wealth creation, I will impact not only their lives but also the lives of their children and possibly their heirs for generations. If I can transfer my knowledge and experience to my clients in a way that motivates them to make the changes and commitments necessary to create an investment strategy based on true principles of wealth creation, I am certain I can impact their lives in a way that has profound meaning. If for any reason, this teaching and learning cannot take place, then I am not interested in doing business for the sake of making a sale. The fact that my wife understands and supports this way of doing business, gives me courage to stick to my principles when developing business with new clients.

Because of my philosophy of teaching and learning versus sales, I have deep and meaningful relationships with my clients. We share bonds of common knowledge and beliefs as well as a confidence that the work we do together results in the best plan for creating and managing their wealth. The fact that I only work with clients who are willing to learn and change, does not mean that my clients have to endure lengthy classroom-like lectures, long meetings or that they become financial experts. It means a small commitment of time and an open mind so that my clients understand a few core financial principles.

I experience incredible satisfaction in my work when teaching and learning occurs with clients and I see the transformation that takes place when clients truly have confidence that the financial course they are pursuing is the correct course. It is such a huge contrast for most clients, who have suffered for years, worried about their financial future. Knowing something isn't right and knowing they should do something different, but not knowing what to do. Knowing they have no confidence in the "plan" of an adviser who is nothing more than a "marketing whiz"; the typical financial planner or broker who knows how to get new clients, but who has no education or training in finance or investment. These clients know intuitively that their adviser has no independent knowledge, but is simply a marketing professional parroting the advice of the firm, selling financial products designed to make the company money and not developed specifically for the need of the client. Finally being on the right path, gives my clients a confidence that pervades all aspects of their lives. Seeing this change in my client's lives brings me great joy and is the driving force behind my work. This experience only happens when I teach and my clients learn.

## OVERCOMING FEAR OF FINANCIAL MARKETS

For over twenty years I have been shedding the light of truth on investment management. I have managed money for the ultra-wealthy and for corporations. As part of the Accredited Network, I now have the opportunity to bring this expertise to the average investor as well. This is an exciting prospect. Everyone should have access to the truth about wealth creation and management.

As I have met and worked with new clients, I have noticed a fear common to many investors. So many people live in fear of the financial markets. They listen to news reports of the market going up and down wildly. Some have even experienced losses in retirement or other investment accounts. Of course in most cases, these investors were either going it alone or working with an adviser like I described above. Using my expertise I can show clients from the wealthiest to the beginner that by applying correct principles there is no need to fear the market. I teach clients that we are not investing in "the market"; we are using tried and true research and analysis methods to find companies with true value, companies with the potential to generate excellent returns through growth, regardless of what the market does. Once clients understand, at least in principle, how they are investing, their fear fades and is replaced with the confidence I mentioned earlier; the confidence of knowing with certainty that their wealth creation and management plan is the right plan for them. I have watched this process repeated over and over for more than twenty years. It is a great feeling to know that the advice I am giving is based on true principles and sound practice and that without my help, most clients would never have access to this life-changing knowledge.

## OUR MISSION

The mission of Manning Investment Group, LLC is: to teach clients the truth about wealth creation and management, to provide them with wealth management solutions that give them confidence that together we have created the best plan possible for the maximization of their wealth.

By the time individuals have completed the process of becoming clients of Manning Investment Group, LLC, they will understand clearly why the myths and misinformation upon which their investments have previously been based are incorrect, damaging and wealth-destroying. Further they will have a clear understanding of the true principles that make our process unique. This understanding will give them a confidence they have never experienced; that they have the best possible plan for creating and managing their wealth given their unique, individual, circumstances. When we achieve this state through teaching and learning we will have fulfilled our mission.

I am grateful to be part of the Accredited Network. My pledge is that each client I serve through the Network will receive the most excellent service my firm can provide. You can contact Phil Manning at:

Manning Investment Group, LLC
QI Consulting, LLC
pmanning@theaccreditednetwork.com
Tel. 800-400-5206
Fax 866-316-5826

# CHAPTER 10

# BOYD COOK
### The Strategic CFO, LLC.

*Boyd Cook has been blessed with personality, something many accountants, tax advisors, and business consultants would love to have. One of the greatest tests in this life is that of stewardship. Cook creates strategies which utilize true accounting principles to assist individuals in accounting for all they have stewardship over. Cook knows that true assets are people and that there will one day be an accounting of all actions. This knowledge is what has separated Cook from other accountants. He has been a real estate investor, a business owner, a tax preparer, a business consultant, a chief financial officer, a controller, and most importantly, he is now, a producer. Combined, these positions have led to a program which will provide the tools to find and create the law of abundance in life. Boyd Cook is the majority owner of more than eight business consulting and accountability practices. He has been personally assisting Garrett Gunderson for over seven years, and he lives the principals of a producer.*

*To receive a free information sheet on how you can begin a program which creates kinetic energy and places you on a path that maximizes your time, unique abilities, and production, please refer to the information bellow.*

*The Strategic CFO, LLC 9890 South 300 West*
*Sandy, Utah 84070*
*bcook@theaccreditednetwork.com*
*888-400-4236*

## L. BOYD COOK

L. Boyd Cook, together with one of my companies, The Strategic CFO, LLC, am transforming the accounting world. I am a dynamic, enthusiastic, creative, and inspiring Personal CFO, if those words can be used to describe a tax accountant. The individual accounting world is ominously deserving of a revolution, a transforming from consumption to production accounting. The Strategic CFO continues to lead the profession to higher and exciting levels of maximization and stewardship of true assets.

At a very young age, I went to the neighborhood store to buy some Swedish Fish. This was a time when you could buy as many or as few Swedish Fish as you wanted. Little did I know that while purchasing these Swedish Fish, I was opening the door to my future as a tax accountant. I walked into a small convenient store that sat in the heart of a rural town in Northern Utah. I opened the pockets of my flood worn Levis to discover I had fourteen pennies. This was not enough to fill my belly before supper, but it was enough to satisfy my sweet tooth. I carefully picked out the fourteen largest Swedish Fish I could find, making certain to handle every other Swedish Fish in the box, and walked to the counter. When I got to the counter I laid the fish down and then reached for my pennies. While doing so the clerk said, "That will be fifteen cents." Trying to understand what the lady had just said, I looked at her in a daze. "Sales Tax," the cashier said reading my thoughts. Still, I looked at her dumbfounded. "You will have to put some back," the clerk finally said. Not really understanding, I counted the fish as I headed back to the box. Sure enough, there were fourteen Swedish Fish. Deciding I might as well save some money for later, as most accountants would have done, I put ten fish back and headed again to the counter. This time I waited for the clerk who said, "That will be four cents, please." Even more confused then ever, I put four cents on the counter and started to walk away when the clerk said, "There is no sales tax on purchases that small." In that exact moment, my young mind started racing as it does today when I meet with clients. I realized that if I purchased four fish, then four more, then four more, and so on, I would never have to pay sales tax on these fish. This may seem like a funny story, however, this is the same approach I take today with my clients. I thoroughly enjoy assisting others in saving taxes.

I love assisting others to maximize their tax savings, but my real passion is in serving and educating others. I graduated with a Masters in Accounting from Utah State University where I served in many leadership positions. I began working at a small firm in the same valley I grew up in, and I have been in the tax and business consulting field for more than nine years. I strongly believe in being a good steward over that which I have been blessed with, and I love assisting others to do the same. I do so through implementing accounting and producer principals together. As will be apparent in greater detail below, my greatest love is watching others learn truth. My one desire is that all could see my heart, understand my passion, cultivate my ideas, and maximize their own wealth, knowledge and Soul Purpose that all may live in the law of abundance and none would go without. For a one page information sheet on my unique production accounting and tax saving process, please email me to or call me at:

bcook@theaccreditednetwork.com

888-400-4236

## ABOUT MY SOUL PURPOSE

My Soul Purpose is to assist others in discovering information they did not already know. There is so much information, on any topic. One can learn almost anything they put their mind, time and effort to. Information is so readily available to people today; this is truly an informational age, an age where knowledge comes so easy, but where knowledge is taken so much for granted. One of my favorite quotes is by philosopher Soren Aabye Kierkegaard who said, "People demand freedom of speech to make up for the freedom of thought which they avoid." Avoiding one's thoughts and not thinking before acting could be one of the most self damning issues facing society today. By surrounding myself with other individuals I find as assets, I can then act on my thoughts. I utilize other individuals so that I can maximize my thoughts and take action on those thoughts. To educate is to empower. Education give you the power to do what one desires and in a way one desires to do it. Knowledge is the power to create, and to create is to produce, and the ability to produce more then one consumes is the ability to achieve financial, spiritual, mental, physical, and social freedom.

## ACCOUNTING FOR MY LIFE

With a Soul Purpose to inspire the world through educating individuals, families, communities, and nations of the power of stewardship and in order for me to be a good steward, I must account for all aspects of my life. My Soul Purpose is to teach others of the "accounting trap" and to assist others in discovering the "savings dilemma," which is to say, individuals, families, communities, and nations can suffer by focusing so much on savings that they fail to focus on production and how best to maximize production. I have a duty and obligation to share with any who will listen the knowledge I have, and this is my Soul Purpose.

I discovered my Soul Purpose at a time I had been thinking about what I enjoy. Spiritually, I have known my Soul Purpose for quite some time, but in the financial realm it took a little longer; to discover something I could do all day any day, was a serious challenge. I had just started my own consulting practice when one day, while attending a Freedom Fast Track meeting, I discovered that my Soul Purpose was something that creates energy for me and others. I focused on my career and the things I enjoyed about it; the things that created energy for me. Then I looked at those moments I was in a state of creation and determined the times I was creating energy and excitement for me as well as for my clients.

Some may ask, "Is it difficult to follow your Soul Purpose after discovering it?" This question can be answered with a question, "Was I an accountant?" Being taught all of my life to live as a natural skeptic, sure it is a challenge to put off my scarcity and act on my knowledge of abundance; I struggled with that, at some point, daily. That being said, I do not believe—once I realized my passions and Soul Purpose— that it was hard to follow that energy. Discovering my Soul Purpose was the hard part, but once I did that, it was easy to allow the excitement of that knowledge to direct my path. For me, once I have the knowledge, it is easy to allow those truths to govern and dictate my actions. Truth is not the mere existence of knowledge, but is the opportunity to express ones' character. Knowing the truth of my Soul Purpose allows me to become, on a daily basis, at one with my Soul Purpose. Understanding and being one with my Soul Purpose has made it naturally comfortable to follow my purpose.

## A UNIVERSAL LAW

Discovering and following my Soul Purpose has made life-changing differences in my life and in the lives of others. If you are anything like me, you love seeing others smiling and enjoying life. Joy is eternal happiness. By living my Soul Purpose, I create joy in my life and in the lives of others. One of the greatest things about my company, The Strategic CFO, is that it creates a kinetic energy placing my clients on the path that maximizes their time, Soul Purpose, and production.

I often think about my Soul Purpose, how to maximize my blessings and talents, and how to be a good steward over my assets and all that entails. There are so many things to take charge of particularly after I discovered my Soul Purpose. By discovering my Soul Purpose, I must take accountability for the responsibilities which that discovery requires. If anyone who has discovered anything would have just kept it to themselves, then where would the world be? If Christopher Columbus would have kept his discovery to himself, what would have transpired? Someone else may have, eventually, discovered the free world, but it would not have been Christopher Columbus. Not only would he have lost out on that discovery, but the discovery itself would have been taken from him. Talents, unique abilities, Soul Purposes, are all things we must be good stewards of. If I am a good steward over my assets, then I will receive more assets. This is an eternal truth, a law that must be followed. Soul Purpose is no different. Once discovered, that Soul Purpose must be utilized in the pursuit of production. The discoverer must be a good steward of that purpose, otherwise, the Soul Purpose may be taken away. This is why I say I have a responsibility and obligation to fulfill my Soul Purposes on all levels.

## THE ABUNDANCE EQUATION

Abundance is having all that one deserves and can be a good steward over. Living the law of abundance does not mean sitting back and letting others create for you and around you. If every person lived their Soul Purpose, the population of the world would be living the law of abundance, meaning everyone would have all they desired. The key is that everyone would be producing more than they were consuming. If production is x, and consumption is y, then the equation would look like this:

$$\text{Number of Assets}(x - y) = \text{Net Production}$$

Therefore, if everyone was living their Soul Purpose, by nature they would be producing more than they were consuming. If everyone's x was more than their y, then the net production would be positive. Thinking about it, if the world had a positive net production then the world would be living in abundance and all would have abundance.

One of my greatest Ah-ha moments came while discovering my Soul Purpose. That Ah-ha came when I realized the only way to have an abundant life was to be a good steward. The Strategic CFO process is designed to assist you in becoming the steward you deserve to be. By living my Soul Purpose and being a good steward over this, I must assist others to do the same. Accounting is, more or less, a snapshot of what has transpired in an entity's financial realm. By taking that accounting, or snapshot, and reviewing it, we can start to become accountable. Being accountable must take place for one to be a good steward. We can make an accounting of all assets, not just monetary assets. For instance, as a tax preparer in today's world, how much faster can I prepare a tax return than someone fifty years ago? With a computer and all of the information available to me, I can prepare a tax return at least ten times faster than a person could have completed the same tax return fifty years ago. Understanding the value the computer is generating, I must be accountable for the time the computer has generated for me. I must make an accounting of that time to be a good steward of it. Utilities are items, possessions, relationships, thoughts, and feelings that can be utilized for production. Time is definitely a utility, and the computer has generated time for me. I can determine what kind of a producer I have been by discovering what I have done with the utilities I have, by taking an accounting of my stewardships, and by verifying that I have produced more then I have consumed.

## UTILIZING HUMAN LIFE VALUE

I have discovered my Soul Purpose, yet I still have to make constant decisions. Knowing and understanding that the only true asset is the value of human life is the key. Utilization of Human Life Value assists me in maximizing my Soul Purpose. Assets are things that have value and can be productive tools, tools of utility. Because all things are created from the world and people, the only true assets are humans, and therefore, Human Life Value is the only true asset.

When I am living my Soul Purpose I am living a life based on true principles. When living a life based on true principles it is not difficult to make decisions the rest of the world may consider difficult. I base my decisions on human life value in conjunction with my Soul Purpose. By striving to maximize my Soul Purpose and utilizing it in the pursuit of valuing others, I am making decisions based on true principles.

By utilizing and maximizing my Soul Purpose, The Strategic CFO will be a leader in the future way of accounting and tax services. Once I discovered my Soul Purpose I had no excuses but to produce. By focusing on my Soul Purpose and putting my energy into my Soul Purpose, I know my companies will continue to thrive. I have also discovered that by assisting others to discover and focus on their Soul Purpose I can better serve in my Soul Purpose. I have surrounded myself with people who know their Soul Purpose and do all they can to maximize that purpose. By allowing others to focus on their Soul Purpose, I am allowed to do the same. This is the key to building a successful business – multiple  individuals all focusing on their Soul Purpose in conjunction with each other.

As I focus on my Soul Purpose and assist in allowing others to focus on their Soul Purpose, I am inspired. Watching others gain excitement for the future as well as the now is very inspiring. This is why my Soul Purpose is to assist others in discovering new information. This is what inspires and creates energy for me: seeing others find and discover new things and watching them become excited and full of energy themselves. This is why I do what I do. This is the purpose of the Strategic CFO. And this is what I like best about what I do.

## THE VISION

My vision is to assist others in discovering the tools they deserve to focus on with their own Soul Purpose. The Strategic CFO goes beyond my clients' financial and physical abilities and places them in a state of creation. While progressing through The Strategic CFO process my clients will discover and find ways to create time and resources which will maximize their net worth, liability protection, and unique abilities. The Strategic CFO process includes seven major steps and is then followed-up with quarterly accountability meetings.  The process begins by setting up a personalized program that will provide asset protection, net worth production, tax savings, and a way to be accountable for stewardships. Then you continue down the path of accountability by meeting quarterly to assure your plan evolves with you and that we are achieving prosperity by design; meaning you are creating prosperity intentionally and in accordance with your plan. By following this process you are allowing The Strategic CFO team the opportunity to focus on their unique abilities while taking anything that creates negative energy away. This will allow our clients to focus on their Soul Purpose and that which brings purpose to and inspires them.

The Strategic CFO process assists clients to live in their Soul Purpose by taking them through seven stages; these steps begin the transformation from consumption to production accounting. This process will give its clients a proactive approach to accounting and taxes which will set them free. These are:

### 1. The Accounting Trap – Discovering the Savings' Dilemma

The Strategic CFO will assist its clients to discover that what is manifested in their life is the same as their focus. For clients that have been raised and taught to hide their talents, as well as those that just want to become better stewards, this stage will take them down the road that will make them the steward they deserve to be.

Accounting traditionally is viewing what has happened. Corporations take what has been accounted for and utilize it to maximize their resources. The Strategic CFO will do the same for each of their clients. In the business world, there are three ways to fund a business: debt offering, equity offering, or contributed capital. The Strategic CFO will utilize the same techniques used in corporate accounting for your personal finances. Sometimes companies need to utilize more debt, sometimes companies need to receive more money from their owners, sometimes companies need to reduce expenses and sometimes companies need to increase their expenses.

By taking the corporate accounting approach on individuals, The Strategic CFO will assist clients to maximize their Net Production which is to say, The Strategic CFO will assist in maximizing ones Soul Purpose.

### 2. The Resource Cultivator – Capturing True Wealth

Wealth is a measurement of one's life, as a whole. It is not the mere existence of or lack of monetary possessions. During this step, The Strategic CFO will capture clients' assets and bring them to total utility.

This stage is designed to capture true wealth. True wealth maximization of human life value; and therefore, true wealth is living an abundant life. An abundant life is living a life of good stewardship. True freedom is the ability to act on choices; therefore, the more I have, the more freedom I have, in all aspects of life. If I am blessed with something and I am a good steward over that something, then I will be blessed with more and the cycle continues. The more I have to be a steward over, the more freedom I enjoy. Here is an example. If I want to go boating right now but I have no boat, am I free to make that choice? Well sure, I can make a choice to go boating, but that does not mean I can go boating. This is how true laws bring freedom as well. If we cling to and follow true principals, then we will, by nature, be good stewards. If we are good stewards, then we will be living an abundant life and therefore a life of more freedom.

This stage of the process will assist The Strategic CFO clients to understand that true wealth is living their Soul Purpose and that the only real assets are people and relationships.

### 3. The Maximization Map – From Reactive to Proactive

Here The Strategic CFO will map out clients individual accounting and tax saving structure. Each individual is unique as is their accounting and tax plan. This map will allow clients to be a producer to its fullest meaning while keeping them in a state of total creation.

### 4. The Cash Flow Generator – Reducing and Producing

Now that clients have their map, the burdens of a reactive approach will be replaced with the comfort of focusing on their unique abilities. Now that The Strategic CFO has created freedom in some areas, The Strategic CFO will assist clients in turning that freedom into production.

### 5. The Accounting Accountability Transformation – Prosperity by Design

We will utilize the prior stages of the Strategic CFO process to transform from a consumption to a production accounting structure. This will allow clients to achieve prosperity in all aspect of their life.

### 6. Transcending Complexity – Breaking the Accounting Barrier

By freeing clients mind, time, talents, abilities, and worth, The Strategic CFO will now transcend the complexity of accounting and taxes and put clients on the road that leads through their new map.

### 7. A New Journey – The End of the Beginning

These stages are only the beginning. The Strategic CFO will continue to educate clients and follow up with them to assure their plan and structure evolves as they progress.

After a decade of working in the accounting world I have discovered many of the frustrations, excitements, services, desires, dilemmas, and needs of individuals as they relate to the accounting and tax profession. With that experience I have put together The Strategic CFO which brings freedom and places clients in a state of total production. This process goes beyond financial and physical abilities and places clients in a state of total creation. This process is for those that are attracting the law of abundance in their life.

The Strategic CFO is part of the Accredited Network. The Accredited Network is one of the greatest inspirations of this age. It is a network of individuals focused on their Soul Purpose and the Soul Purpose of others. Being a part of the Accredited Network means that I have unique abilities in my specific field. Those unique abilities are utilized and brought to pass as I live my Soul Purpose. The Accredited Network is just that, a network. By allowing others to focus on their Soul Purpose, which everyone in the Accredited Network does, I can focus on my Soul Purpose, and as a whole, we all benefit and live in the law of abundance.

As part of my vision for The Strategic CFO, I want to leave a legacy of simplicity. The vision of The Strategic CFO is to progress to the point where all of The Strategic CFO clients are constantly focusing on their Soul Purpose. The Strategic CFO will take on the role of a personal accounting department. The Strategic CFO will assign clients a bookkeeper, a tax specialist, an entity specialist, a payroll department, and their own personal CFO (chief financial officer). By doing this The Strategic CFO will take a proactive approach to clients accounting and tax needs saving them thousands of dollars and more importantly, allowing them to maximize their Soul Purpose.

I would be honored to meet with you. My clients enhance my life and my business, as well as provide me with the opportunity to do all I can to assist them in maximizing their Soul Purpose. Take action and start your proactive and producer approach to accounting and taxes by getting in touch with The Strategic CFO.

# TAKE ACTION NOW
## DON'T WAIT OR HESITATE. ANSWER THE FOLLOWING QUESTIONS

**What was the single, most important idea you got from this chapter?**

_____

_____

_____

_____

**How will this idea help you reach your Soul's Purpose?**

_____

_____

_____

_____

**What steps will you take immediately to insure you follow through with you new insight?**

_____

_____

_____

_____

**What is one question you would like answered regarding The Strategic CFO?**

_____

_____

_____

_____

# CHAPTER 11

# DANE MILLER
### Foundations insurance

*Dane Miller was born on January 29, 1974 in Bountiful, Utah. He currently resides in Lehi, Utah with his wife Dawn and three children (2 girls and a boy).*

*Dane received his Bachelors of Science degree in Exercise and Sports Science from the University of Utah in 1999.*

*In his spare time Dane enjoys spending time with his family, traveling and anything involving sports. Dane was a Cross Country/Track runner in college and is now competing in Triathlons.*

*Dane started working in the Accredited Network with Foundations Insurance in February 2007. Before this he had about nine years of experience in the Insurance Industry in both agencies and as an auto claims adjuster.*

**Contact Information:**
*Dane Miller*
*Protection Specialist/Agent*
*Foundations Insurance*
*9890 South 300 West, Suite 300*
*Office Phone: 800-400-5206*
*E-mail: dmiller@theaccreditednetwork.com*

## IDENTIFYING SOUL PURPOSE

Identifying one's Soul Purpose often requires trial and error in a variety of occupations that are closely related to that perfect expression of self, but do not precisely tap into the combination of ability, passion, and meaning at the very foundation of Soul Purpose. It may take many years of experimentation and exploration in various jobs or entrepreneurial ventures before Soul Purpose is achieved in any meaningful way. When Soul Purpose is found, however, the extra work required to achieve it is made all that much more worthwhile.

Living your Soul Purpose results in complete fulfillment within a profession that is personally challenging, inspiring, and rewarding. In the following pages, I will describe my own path to Soul Purpose, the fulfillment of that Soul Purpose through his current work as a Protection Specialist with Foundations Insurance, and the process through which I take my clients in order to protect assets despite unavoidable risk.

My Soul Purpose is to teach and educate people about the Principles of Protection. These are fundamental, timeless, and unchanging natural laws that govern risk and risk management in human life. These laws exist whether or not we know about them, or believe in them. They are like gravity, in that they respond immediately to a person's actions, and execute the consequences (positive or negative) of those actions.

I express my Soul Purpose as a Protection Specialist with Foundations Insurance, walking clients through a unique process that teaches them The Principles of Protection, and implements a comprehensive Asset Protection Plan that establishes financial certainty regardless of future circumstance. More importantly, this Asset Protection Plan helps clients maintain a Mindset of Abundance, a key to living The Producer Paradigm. By understanding and implementing the Principles of Protection, clients can maximize the production of their resources, and utilize them for the activities, aspirations, and ambitions that truly bring joy to their lives. My Soul Purpose, ultimately, is to teach clients how to create that joy.

## FINDING SOUL PURPOSE THROUGH WORK EXPERIENCES

My Soul Purpose journey began when I started working in my father's State Farm Insurance agency at the age of 21. Between my time there, and work done at another agency during college, I already had four-and-a-half years of insurance experience by the time I graduated from college.

After college I completed an internship with State Farm, working in roughly 30 different agencies, observing their business practices and helping to consolidate client records to prepare for the rollout of a new software system. From this work, I learned the most effective methods for running an insurance agency, and began to identify The Principles of Protection that now guide my own education of clients.

I then worked for three-and-a-half years as a Claims Adjuster for State Farm, evaluating bodily injury and property damage claims. During this time I settled hundreds of claims ranging from minor automobile damage to bodily injury claims involving death.

For reasons I describe in greater detail below, I then took a job as an Exercise Technician and Manager of America's Back & Neck Clinic, a spine rehabilitation center in Denver, CO. During my three-and-a-half years there, I educated people on and implemented exercise therapy programs to help people suffering from back and neck pain.

Currently, I work as a Protection Specialist for Foundations Insurance, fulfilling my Soul Purpose as I educate people on the Principles of Protection and help them to implement policies based on these principles.

## HOW I DISCOVERED MY SOUL PURPOSE

I'm sometimes asked how I discovered my Soul Purpose. During my time as a Claims Adjuster with State Farm, I was exposed to countless people who had lost physical assets, or been injured in accidents for which they had no insurance coverage. Quite simply, these people didn't have insurance when they needed it, or didn't have enough insurance to cover the damages resulting from their accidents.

In some ways, having too little insurance was worse than having none at all. People with too little insurance suffered insult piled on top of injury. They expected the damages from their accidents to be covered, but often ended up in financial ruins as devastating as those without insurance at all. In both instances people's lives were turned upside down physically, emotionally and financially.

Through this work, I gained an understanding of the difference between the "price" and the "cost" of adequate asset protection. In this way, I viewed my work as a Claims Adjuster from a much different perspective than Insurance Agents or other professionals view their work. I participated in the process used to determine, both in dollars and in Human Life Value, how much accidents cost the individuals involved.

As a Claims Adjuster I became very interested in the rehabilitation accident victims went through after their injuries. Many people involved in accidents have ongoing back and neck problems. I had always had an interest in Physical Therapy, and so I decided to pursue a greater understanding of the intersection between accidents, insurance, and injury rehabilitation.

I moved to Denver, CO and began managing a group of Spine Rehabilitation clinics. During my three-and-a-half years in this industry I was able to help many people dealing with back and neck problems resulting from car accidents and other injuries.

My work with sufferers of back and neck pain further exposed me to the problem of inadequate insurance coverage. Many of the patients at the Spine Rehabilitation clinics I managed were paying for our services out-of-pocket, or racking up thousands of dollars in credit card debt to get some form of relief from their pain. Many people completed only a partial course of treatment until their insurance benefits ran out, at which time they quit their rehabilitation, and lost any progress they had made toward ending their suffering.

Exposure to these unlucky and unprepared patients convinced me even more of the infinite value of insurance coverage when it is needed. The difference between the "price" of insurance and the "cost" of not having it (or enough of it) was hammered home every time I said goodbye to a patient knowing he or she needed additional care.

This was frustrating to me. Even though I had changed careers, and began serving accident victims in a whole new way through my work at the Spine Rehab clinics, I still faced the same dilemma. Often I couldn't give an accident victim needed care, because there was no way to pay for it.

I became passionate about encouraging people to protect their health, wealth, assets, and Human Life Value through adequate insurance coverage. After three-and-a-half years managing Spine Rehab clinics, I made the discovery of my true passion, educating people on a set of Principles which had been developing in my mind through years of experience helping accident victims.

In order to effectively educate people on the Principles of Protection, a person must be on the "front lines" of the insurance industry, meeting with clients and teaching them about risk, risk management, and the "cost" of inadequate insurance coverage compared to the "price" of the coverage itself. The person who does this is the Insurance Agent.

From my own experience in the industry, I believe that very few Insurance Agents understand the responsibility they bear to educate their clients on adequate coverage. Many Insurance Agents see themselves as salespeople. Others view their role as an advisor, but lack the interpersonal or communication skills to teach clients. Some few Insurance Agents have both the understanding and the ability to teach, but have never bothered to create a formal process that educates clients in a consistent, ongoing way.

I have always considered myself a good teacher, and get great personal satisfaction out of sharing my knowledge with others. When I decided to leave my work in Spine Rehabilitation, I realized that teaching others about the Principles of Protection as an Insurance Agent was a natural fit for my personality, abilities, and passions.

Initially, I investigated the possibility of opening up a State Farm agency of my own. My father had been a lifelong State Farm agent, and I believe the company offers good, trustworthy products. At the same time, however, my brother Darron Miller (CEO of Foundations Insurance) quit his State Farm agency to start Foundations. After discussions with him, I realized that his philosophy for Foundations was based on the same Principles of Protection I had come to understand for myself. We committed to work together toward a common mission: "To educate clients on the Principles of Protection to help them make the best decision on their Insurance Coverage."

Once I realized the impact I could have on people's lives through my work with Foundations, the decision to move my family from Colorado to Utah was easy.

Through this work, I'm able to teach and educate people every single day about the Principles of Protection. I'm able to help people understand the true value of insurance as a tool of financial certainty, production, and the Abundance Mindset.

## WHAT FOUDATIONS INSURANCE OFFERS

The education I provide clients is formal, in that it covers specific topics that are fundamental to understanding the Principles of Protection. However, we cover these topics in an informal setting and manner, giving the client the opportunity to determine the pace of the learning, and ask questions.

The fundamental objective of the process is to teach the client "why" the price of insurance is always less than the costs associated with not having it. The "why" of insurance is probably the least understood component of a comprehensive financial blueprint. Until a Producer understands why insurance is an essential part of establishing financial freedom, he will not be able to maximize the production of his resources.

As part of this conversation, the client and I identify what and whom insurance is meant to protect. We analyze the client's current insurance coverage to determine whether or not the policy is accomplishing their reasons for buying insurance (their why). If their current coverage doesn't achieve these objectives, we discuss, discover, and implement policies that help them accomplish their reasons.

## WHAT VALUE DO I SHARE WITH OTHERS?

I teach the importance of making insurance coverage decisions using a Principle-Based Strategy instead of just strategy based on experience.

Most policies are designed using a strategy based on experience. Coverage is selected to insure against events that have happened in a person's past. People think that, if their coverage was adequate in the past, the same coverage will be adequate always. A variation of this thinking is to select coverage that insures against statistically significant risks, the most likely outcome of an accident. Still others simply base their insurance coverage on what most people get.

These are all ineffective strategies that typically leave people underinsured. People use these strategies because they have been taught to buy insurance using inappropriate logic, and wrong priorities. This logic convinces them to buy insurance because they "might" have an accident, they "might" get sick, or something else "might" happen. Anytime a policy is designed this way, coverage is based on guesswork. Guessing provides no greater surety than the risk associated with having an accident itself. A person guessing at the amount of insurance to buy "might" not have enough insurance, just as easily as they "might" get in an accident. This goes against the most fundamental "why" of buying insurance in the first place, to establish certainty for the future.

So, what is "adequate protection?" How much insurance is enough? The only way to answer this is to know the dollar amount of the damages of one's future accidents, and buy precisely that much insurance coverage. Is the ridiculousness of this proposition obvious? The truth is that we can never know the exact amount of insurance we will need. By the very nature of risk, we cannot predict the time, place, seriousness, or dollar amount of damage from an accident.

Because we never know the amount of damage caused by an accident until after it has occurred, most people just make a guess based on their own past experience, on statistics, or on the common coverage purchased, and design their insurance policy according. Sadly for many people with such coverage, the past is not always an accurate predictor of the future, statistics only provide an average of accident damages, and commonly purchased policies leave their owners woefully underinsured. In my work as a Claims Adjuster and a Spine Rehab Clinic manager, I met countless numbers of people who had designed their insurance policies with this faulty logic, and were left underinsured and unprotected when the damages from their accidents exceeded their coverage.

The Principle-Based Strategy I teach clients is to buy insurance to manage the inherent unpredictability of the risks they face in life.

There are only three ways to manage any type of risk, whether it is the risk to our vehicles and bodies from driving our car, the risk to our property and assets from owning our homes, the risk to our money from owning businesses, or the risk to our safety from being human and venturing out into the dangerous world every day. We can (1) try to AVOID risks, (2) RETAIN risks, or (3) TRANSFER risks.

It is nearly impossible to avoid the majority of the risks we face in life. For example, no matter how carefully we drive, the risks a person is exposed to from driving do not come exclusively from their own driving ability or attentiveness. Poor or distracted drivers place other drivers at risk as well. We simply have no control over other drivers on the road.

Some might conclude that the only way to avoid the risks of driving are to not drive. This might be true to a certain extent. But, whatever alternate means of transportation one chooses have their own risks. And, if a person stays home all day to avoid the risks of driving, the costs of being a hermit are probably not worth the additional safety one gets from abandoning society. In fact, there are just as many risks at home as there are on the streets. No matter where we go, or what we do, we face unavoidable risk. Because we can't avoid these risks, we must either retain them or transfer them.

When we retain risk we keep it ourselves. Either we don't buy any insurance to cover these risks, or we don't buy enough insurance to adequately compensate for damages and losses that occur from the risk. Remember that it is impossible to know the amount of damage, in dollars, that will result from an accident. Therefore, any amount of retained risk resulting from inadequate coverage might result in truly devastating financial consequences.

Risk is transferred by paying an insurance company to assume the financial consequences of an accident for us. Let's use the risks associated with home ownership as an example: Say you have a $400,000 home. For whatever reason, it is insured for $300,000. In this example, the risk, in dollars, is the value of the home or $400,000. If it is insured for $300,000, that is the amount of risk transferred to the insurance company. If the house burned down, the insurance company would pay up to $300,000 to rebuild the home. This leaves $100,000 retained by the homeowner. After the house burns down, if it does take $400,000 to rebuild, the homeowner will have to come up with the $100,000 that was not transferred. Where is the $100,000 going to come from? If the homeowner doesn't have the money in the bank or some investment that he can liquidate, the house is either never rebuilt, or rebuilt on a $300,000 budget. The homeowner is not "made whole" for the loss. If the homeowner does have the money, there is still a loss resulting from its use to rebuild the property. The "opportunity cost" is the future use of that money.

No matter what situation you run through the above exercise, anytime you RETAIN any amount of risk, the cost is always higher than the price of TRANSFERING the risk to an insurance company. Understanding this is the key to making a Principle-Based decision about insurance coverage. We cannot AVOID risk, but we can protect ourselves from risk by transferring it to an insurance company.

Consider for a moment: If you knew you were going to be in an automobile accident tomorrow, but you didn't know how much damage was going to be caused, how much insurance would you get today? As much as possible, right?

Knowing that you are taking on risk everyday when you get in your car, take the bus, live in your house, or walk outside of it, and knowing that the potential damage, in dollars, from these risks is unpredictable, how much of that risk do you want to transfer to an insurance company? Just like the case above, the answer should be "As Much as Possible.

The key to the Principles of Protection is this simple understanding of risk transfer: AS MUCH AS POSSIBLE. You see, when we get as much insurance as possible, there is no guessing involved. You are doing all you can to protect your assets. You are decreasing your uncertainty to as close to zero as possible. This is Principle-Based Protection.

## THE GUIDING PRINCIPLES I USE IN LIFE AND BUSINESS

When evaluating the Principles of Protection, there are a few of the more expansive Principles of Prosperity outlined in the Producer Revolution that stand out. These are the Principles that Darron Miller and I discussed when Foundations Insurance was first created, and which are still discussed everyday at Foundations.

### Agency Implies Stewardship

Anytime we get into our vehicles, and every day we live in our homes, we are taking on the responsibility that goes with the ownership of those pieces of property. We choose to drive, so we have a stewardship over the consequences if we cause damage. Do we have stewardship only over most of the damage we might cause? No, we have stewardship over all of it. We are proper stewards when we insure for as many situations as possible, including situations where our actions result in damage to others.

Imagine you get home from work today and your neighbor is standing on your front porch with one of your children. Your neighbor informs you that your ten year old child has stolen $1,000 from him. Your first reaction might be to deny it, but imagine for the sake of this example that your child, in fact, admits to having taken the money. How would you handle the situation?

Most people would require the child to repay the money. Imagine that you make such a demand, and your child says that the money is already spent. What then? Many people would then require that the child work to repay the stolen money. But, at this time the neighbor demands that the much-needed money be repaid immediately. As a guardian for your children, you are largely responsible for the effects of their actions on other people. Most people in this situation would repay the neighbor, and then require the child to work off the debt in some way. This is similar to insurance. In this situation, the parent is the insurance company, the neighbor is the claimant and the child is the insured.

In situations where you could not repay the cost of damages caused by your actions, insurance is the only way to be a good steward over your social commitments to others. Even if you could repay the damages caused by accidents for which you are at fault, it would be poor financial prioritizing to put your money at risk instead of an insurance company's.

### People Are Assets

Most of the people I speak with about insurance initially give one of two common reasons for buying insurance. Some people say they buy insurance because they are legally required to. I always chuckle at this reasoning, because it is extremely short-sighted. After discussing insurance with these clients for less than two minutes, they usually admit that they actually buy insurance for the second reason, given by nearly all other clients: protection.

Once people realize that insurance is purchased for protection, the important question to answer is: What does insurance protect?

Roughly speaking, all things of value can be classified as assets. Insurance is there to protect our assets. As an exercise in the Principles of Protection, spend a minute to make a list of your assets. Are any of the assets you listed not protected by some sort of insurance policy? Which of the assets you wrote down is your most important asset?

For Producers who understand the source and nature of wealth creation, other people are the most important asset. Without other people, production in all areas of life goes to zero.

Insurance is there to protect the policy owner, but is also there to ensure that other people are made whole if the policy owner causes damage to them. This recognition of other people as the true assets in life, and commitment to treating other people as assets by protecting them against damage we cause, is the hallmark of the Producer Paradigm.

## MY "AHA" MOMENT

I lived in Colorado when 2 of the original partners of Engenuity (Les McGuire and Ray Hooper) were killed in a plane crash. Les is my cousin, so I came in for the funeral and spent a great deal of time at Utah Lake while rescuers searched for their bodies. I met many of the people involved with Les and Ray in Engenuity, and The Producer Revolution. I learned of the amazing work Les and Ray had been doing to bring the Principles of Prosperity to others, and the ongoing commitment that Garrett Gunderson, Mike Isom, and others had to keep their legacy alive.

At that time I had no plans of moving from Colorado. But, from the conversations I had during my time in Utah, I realized that something was missing in my life. I went back to Colorado determined to be a part of this network of people, even if I lived in a different state. I joined the Producer Revolution and started reading and studying books and materials that were recommended. After reading Atlas Shrugged and Rich Dad, Poor Dad, I made the decision to move.

Becoming a member of the Producer Revolution and striving to live by the Principles of Prosperity has been my greatest Ah-ha moment. The changes that have taken place in my mind and thoughts have totally altered my life and the results I'm getting in life.

## MAKING DIFFICULT DECISIONS

Principles govern. Any decision made on principle is a good decision. When faced with a difficult decision, I try to identify the principles governing that area of life, align my values to those principles and move forward accordingly.

## MY INSPIRATION

I'm inspired by many things. My family and my desire to give them the best life possible inspires me. My friends and all they bring into my life inspire me to give more back to them. Big dreams inspire me to never settle for mediocrity. Overcoming long-term, difficult obstacles inspires me to break through the daily barriers on the path to accomplishing these larger objectives. Achieving things that others think aren't possible or reasonable inspires me. Living an unreasonable life inspires me.

## WHY I DO IT

As I mentioned earlier, my experiences as a Claims Adjuster and manager of Spine Rehab Clinics opened my eyes to the devastation caused by lack of insurance. I saw a big problem that inspired me to get involved on the front lines of finding a solution. I educate people on the Principles of Protection to help them avoid the financial, emotional, physical, and spiritual suffering that comes from ignoring these principles.

## WHY I LOVE IT

I love teaching and educating people. I love sharing the knowledge I've gained from my own experiences, to create valuable insight for others. The Accredited Network has opened my eyes to a whole new realm of possibility and productivity that I never knew existed. I work with amazing people from the Accredited Network every day. My Human Life Value has increased tremendously through these associations. What greater thing is there than to increase your own ability to create value for others? I want to be remembered as someone who contributed to the growth and productivity of others. I want my commitment to being an excellent husband, father, son, friend, boss, and associate to live on in the difference I made in the lives of those I love.

## A CALL TO ACTION

If you aren't certain that you understand the Principles of Protection, or know that you haven't adequately implemented them in your insurance policies, I would love to sit down with you. I guarantee that you won't find the education-oriented process I provide clients through any other insurance company. I work to understand your personal reasons for buying insurance and whether your current coverage fulfills these reasons. I am committed to the well-being of every client with whom I work, and to ensuring that their most important assets are protected against any possible risk. *Call me for an appointment @ 800-400-5206.*

# CHAPTER 12

# CONCLUSION
### By Garrett B. Gunderson

I hope that you, the reader, have truly recognizd how valuable and unique this collection of personal experiences and insights is. I hope that you realized this, so that you can fully appreciate and absorb some of the many insights and incredible wisdom contained in these pages. I hope that you also relalized how remarkable and gifted each of these Producers are, so that you can benefit from association with them as well. I have invested tens of thousands of dollars attending seminars, programs and events. I have spent years of my own time and efforts to be taught by the very best, but I sincerely would love for you to be able to build upon on my efforts and be that much further ahead in your own life. If you are looking to surround yourself with a team of individuals who can help you maximize your own Soul Purpose, wealth, and abundance in every sense of the word, then you now have in your hands the tool to do so. Each of these contributors shared their contact information somewhere near the end of their chapter and there is a card that can be mailed in to express interest in any program mentioned. If you haven't already, I would recommend mailing in the card and marking any area of interest that you have to schedule appointments with any of these Producers or their organizations that you believe could help you take your life to the next level. Each of these individuals has already done that for me, and are continuing to do so.

If you would like to personally meet some of the individuals in this book, and be tutored by some of the finest Producers in the world, then I invite you to The Big Event sponsored by Freedom FastTrack. This event is our annual three-day flagship symposium. Renowned and world famous individuals will personally teach you the keys to prosperity in every Track of Human Life Value: Financial, Spiritual, Mental, Physical and Social. These incredible, high-level mentors will help you discover the disciplines, strategies and techniques to uncover and resolve any obstacle, while also permanently increasing your joy, health and prosperity in life. The creators of each FastTrack program, the absolute experts of their craft who have dedicated their lives to understanding these principles, will also share their hard-earned enlightenment to save you years of frustrating trial and error. In a nutshell, this event provides the most exciting, rejuvenating and expansive experience of a lifetime.

You will experience the comprehensive philosophies and practices behind every major realm of life:

**Financial-** Discover how to turn latent potential and inactive resources into production. What things do you need to know to get rid of fear permanently, so you get beyond the excuses and enjoy the freedom. See what's possible for you. Understand certainty and cash flow versus risk and accumulation.

**Soul Purpose-** This portion will uncover the obstacles keeping from you living your ideal life, and realize how to become an enlightened creator. The disciplines, the strategies and techniques of living your dream life will be powerfully revealed. You will learn how to make these discoveries keep you motivated throughout your entire lifetime.

**Mental-** Learn how to unlock the genius within, and how to master the ability to choose abundance in the face of scarcity. Gain an understanding of the system for creating more powerful thoughts that provide the framework for transformation. Uncover blind spots, and learn how to engage constantly from your most powerful plane of potential, so that your inner abundance can be reflected onto the outside world.

**Physical-** Receive the tools to engage and initiate successful plans. Dispel the misinformation about nutrition. You will also learn how to increase you metabolic rate, avoid sickness, and enjoy peak physical performance. Learn how the physical realm can increase productivity in every other aspect of your life, as you learn the principles of wise stewardship over your physical body. Gain a deeper understanding of how to maximize the powerful connections between mind, body and soul.

**Social-** Learn ways our relationships with others profoundly affect our prosperity. Identify the steps and keys required to experience mutually satisfying relationships both professionally and personally. Gain a deeper understanding of the components that truly bring lasting happiness into our lives. Learn how all of the other Tracks fit into the context of people, and how to create the kind of legacy that not only benefits your posterity, but the entire world.

If you have any questions about this, any other Freedom FastTrack program or event, please contact The Freedom FastTrack at **1-800-549-4532**.

One very common fallacy that too many of us live by is a false concept of "rugged individualism" versus interdependence. Relying too heavily on "rugged individualism" in life is like the hamster that keeps running as hard as it can on it's stationary running wheel. It may be working hard, but it's not going anywhere. More often than not, when we are not progressing financially—or in any other way—it takes the knowledge and gifts of other talented individuals to help us gain a new perspective and see things more clearly. As I have personally found, allowing the Soul Purpose of others to help us get us off of our respective "hamster wheels" and onto exciting new levels of existence, is among the smartest decisions we can make in this life. Are you ready?

# THE ECONOMIC$ OF SOUL PURPOSE

## FROM PASSION TO PRODUCTIVITY

If you are interested in working with any of the contributors in this book, or would like to find out more about how their services can improve your business or personal finances, please check the box next to their name to be contacted.

☐ Garrett B. Gunderson
☐ Garrett White
☐ Steve D'Annunzio
☐ Jason Byrne
☐ Kim Butler
☐ Greg Blackbourn
☐ Philip Tirone
☐ Dee Randall
☐ Phil Manning
☐ Boyd Cook
☐ Dane Miller

Are there any additional books, products, programs or services that you would like to know more about? ☐ YES

To get a free one-month Power Hour Membership visit ProducerPowerHour.com and sign up using the code: Soul Purpose

For other free offers and upcoming events please call (800)400-5206 or email info@theaccreditednetwork.com for more information.

The
**Accredited**
NETWORK™

*Fill out the card below and mail to:* The Accredited Network  9890 South 300 West Suite 301  Sandy, UT 84070

_____
NAME

_____
STREET ADDRESS

_____
CITY                          STATE                          ZIP

_____
EMAIL (OPTIONAL)